The Shepherd's Crook

The Shepherd's Crook

David R. Tullock

To order additional copies of this book, contact:
Xlibris Corporation
1-888-795-4274
www.Xlibris.com
Orders@Xlibris.com
48092

CONTENTS

All I could never be,
All men ignored in me,
This, I was worth to God,
whose wheel the pitcher shaped.

John Greenlief Whittier

FOREWORD

By all accounts, King David should not have been a success as King of Israel. His chronicles reveal more failures than successes, yet by God's account he was a man after God's own heart.

It was David's relation with God that defined his life. More than anything else, David knew where to properly place his sins and successes—with God. That's what we can learn to do from David's example. In spite of our sins, debauches, treachery, and conspiracies David is an example that God has the last word in our stories. God's grace trumps our inadequacies.

This book is a collection of sermons preached to a congregation that I hold in great fondness, First Baptist Church of Rossville, Georgia. I served as their pastor from 1988-1997. They taught me the importance of Whittier's words when he wrote "whose wheel the pitcher made."

Further, I wish I could say that all the ideas for these sermons were original to me. I am especially grateful to Charles Swindoll for prompting the thoughts and preparations of the sermons with his study book, *A Man After God's Own Heart*, and to Ken Chafin, Stephen Shoemaker, Raymond Bailey and Gary Redding for influencing my preaching then and now.

Finally, I dedicate this book to my church family, Northside Presbyterian Church, Cleveland Tennessee, who thoughtfully listen to my sermons and lovingly care for me and my family.

David R. Tullock
2008

A BRAND NEW DAY

II Samuel 1

The beauty Israel is slain upon thy high places: how are the mighty fallen! (II Samuel 1:19)

There was once a young mother who was preparing a ham roast for her family for supper. As she was cooking, her young son was standing beside her observing her actions. In preparing the roast he saw that she cut off the end of the ham. He asked her why she cut the tips of the ham. She said because her mother always did it.

After thinking a moment, she decided to call her mother to ask her why she cut the ham before she cooked it. Her mother said that she cut the ham because her mother always did it that way.

Having her curiosity raised, she called her grandmother and asked her why she cut her ham before she baked it. She said that she cut her ham because her pan was to small for it to fit properly!

Sometimes we find ourselves in a rut and we don't know why we are there. Someone has said that a rut is a grave with both ends knocked out.

Some people are comfortable with change. New fads, new concepts and new ideas capture their imagination. They sit down at 6:00 p.m. or 11:00 p.m to find out what is new. That's why we call it the news. These type of people are easily bored if their surroundings are not changed frequently. If their ideas are not challenged they feel life is dull and monotonous. These people drive a different way to work every day, they seek adventure. Their daily schedule is erratic.

Some people are not comfortable with change. They like the way things used to be. Nostalgia, antiques and history capture their imagination. These type of people do things the same way day in day out. Breakfast at 7:00, lunch a 12:00, dinner at 5:00. They are most comfortable with a routine.

Whether we like it or not, life's main ingredient is change. Our life is not the same as it was yesterday. It may be better or it may be worse but it is not the same. It may be happier or it may be sadder. It may be fuller or it may be emptier. Nevertheless, it is different.

Many times we find ourselves stuck between old and new. Frustrated. Waiting for the happiness we thought we would have when we reached this point in our life.

You are sixteen and you've just received your driver's license and you discover it not what it's cracked up to be. You have finally finished high school or college and you discover there's more to life than a diploma or degree. You're a newly wed and you think you would be happy if you could only have children. Your kids are about to leave the nest and you can't wait to live life again once their gone. You think you'll really find happiness when you get that new job or promotion. If I could only have some grand kids. If I can make it to retirement, then I'll be happy. If . . . If . . . If . . . .

Happiness does not occur then and there; it occurs here and now. We find ourselves struggling between the old days when life was good and the new days when everything will be O.K. and in the meantime we suffocate life with thoughts of what we cannot do rather than the things we can do. We spend our lives focusing on tomorrow while all along today is ignored.

David had been living life between the cracks. No longer in the fields with his father's sheep but not living his new life on the throne of Israel. No longer shepherd but not yet king. David is patiently waiting for God to deliver him into the royal world. What are the principles in this story of David that will help us when we find ourselves in the cracks? Have can we deal with the struggles between the old and the new? How is God working to bring us a brand new day?

The first truth is this—As God ushers in a new day something old must pass away. One period of time must cease before another can begin.

In order for David to assume the throne of Israel, Saul had to die. There could not be two kings in Israel. Even though Saul and David were arch rivals and enemies, it was still difficult for David to hear of Saul's death.

Saul's death marked the end of David's fugitive days. It was finally time for him to be crowned king. Death marks an ending, but it also ushers in a beginning. The seeds of new life are scattered with the ashes of each death.

For example, the death of a parent breeds new responsibilities for a child. A spouse's death breeds a new lifestyle for the mate left behind. A death of a friend means a time of adjustment must begin for the one left behind.

Hearing of Saul's death was very painful for David. He mourned the lose of this anointed one of Israel. He said:

> The beauty Israel is slain upon thy high places: how are the mighty fallen! (II Samuel 1:19)

The second truth is this—As God ushers in a new day we must ask for His timing. We must realize his way for us.

In II Samuel we find that even though David knows he is to be the next king he inquires of the Lord:

> Shall I go up into any of the cities of Judah? And the Lord said: Go Up. And David said unto him. Where shall I go up? And he said unto Hebron. (II Samuel 2:1)

There is a story about a old lady from Scotland who traveled the country side to sell threads, buttons and cloth. When she would come to a fork in the road she would through her walking stick into the air and determine which way to go by where the stick would fall.

One day she came to a fork in the road. One road was smooth and level. The other way rocky and steep. She through her stick and it landed on the rough road. Displeased with traveling the rough road she threw her stick again and again until it fell on the smooth road.

We treat the will of God that way sometimes. We know what we want to do and we finally talk ourselves into doing it as if it were the will of God.

David was asking, "What does God want me to do?" or "What is the right thing to do?" Aren't we sometimes afraid to asked these kinds of questions to God? We are afraid that he will upset our apple cart. He will upset our status quo.

Not long ago a missionary had come home from Africa to bring three of her children so they could go to school in the United States. After she had found homes for them, through the help of the Woman's Missionary Union, and all of the arrangements had been made for their care, she made her reservations to return to Africa. The evening before she left, a group of fine Christian people gave her a farewell reception. One of them said to her, "I am sure you are eager to get back to your mission field."

For a moment there was a frown on the missionary's face and then very solemnly she answered. "No, I am not eager to get back. The place to which I am going is dirty. There are no electric lights, there are no modern conveniences whatsoever. There is no pure water, and I will be cooking on my wood stove, and while I cook I will be weeping because my children are so far away. I will be desperately lonesome for them and wondering if any of them are sick.

"When I remember that it will be three years before I see them again, I will be tempted to tell the Lord that I can't stand it and I am going home. No, I am not eager to return to Africa, but I am more eager to do the Lord's will than to do anything else. I would be more miserable here than there."

The third truth is this—As God ushers in a new day we must allow God to transform the old day into the new day.

When David assumed the throne of Judah, he had many obstacles to conquer. He did not receive the throne automatically or easily. There were several satellite kings that had to be dealt with. Instead of taking things into his own hands, David had to exercise patience and allow God to work. Not only did he ask for God's guidance, he followed God's advise.

Elton Trueblood said that the worst kind of blasphemy is not profanity but lip service. Many times we feel that if we have a Christian vocabulary that we are practicing a Christian lifestyle. Vocabulary and lifestyle are not one in the same.

Hitler knew how to dissemble. One had to look very closely at his terrible book, *Mein Kampf,* to see the difference between his vocabulary and his lifestyle.

He made free use of the Christian vocabulary. He talked about the blessing of the Almighty and the Christian confessions which would become pillars of his new state. He rang bells and pulled out all the organ stops. He assumed the earnestness of a man who is utterly weighed down by historic responsibility. He handed out pious stories to the press, especially the church papers.

It was reported, for example, that he showed his tattered Bible to some deacons and declared that he drew the strength for his great work from the Word of God. He was able to introduce a pietistic timbre into his voice which caused many religious people to welcome him as a man sent from God. And despite a skilled propaganda machine saw to it that despite all the atrocities which were already happening and despite the rabid invasions of the Nazis in the churches, the rumor got around that the "good" Fuhrer knew nothing about these things.

Many of the men of David's day were using religion as a stalking horse for political expedience. They felt that if there words were cloaked in spirituality that David would give them a place in his kingdom. Others employed the will of God for private revenge. We must depend upon God to deal with the old in our life and to make it new. Paul says:

> If any man be in Christ, he is a new creation, old things are passed
> away behold all things become new. (II Corinthians 4:17)

The fourth truth is this—As God ushers in a new day we must avoid a life of self sufficiency and pride. The writer of II Samuel says these words about David:

> And David went on, and grew great, and the Lord God of hosts
> was with him. (II Samuel 5:10)

There was a direct correlation between David's strength and God's presence in his life? The biggest threat to our Christian life is when think we can live life without God. We need to remember that it is not what I want to be or do or what you want to be or to do but what God wants you and me to be or to do.

Do you find yourself struggling between the old and the new? Are you finding it difficult distinguishing between your will and God's will for your life. God wants us to depend on him for our new day, and as He ushers in that new day he will turn our mourning into dancing.

THE OPPORTUNITY OF A LIFETIME

I Samuel 10:1-8

When Samuel became old, he made his sons judges over Israel. The name of his firstborn son was Joel, and the name of his second, Abijah; they were judges in Beer-sheba. Yet his sons did not follow in his ways, but turned aside after gain; they took bribes and perverted justice.

Then all the elders of Israel gathered together and came to Samuel at Ramah, and said to him, "You are old and your sons do not follow in your ways; appoint for us, then, a king to govern us, like other nations." But the thing displeased Samuel when they said, "Give us a king to govern us." Samuel prayed to the Lord, and the Lord said to Samuel, "Listen to the voice of the people in all that they say to you; for they have not rejected you, but they have rejected me from being king over them. Just as they have done to me, from the day I brought them up out of Egypt to this day, forsaking me and serving other gods, so also they are doing to you. Now then, listen to their voice; only—you shall solemnly warn them, and show them the ways of the king who shall reign over them." So Samuel reported all the words of the Lord to the people who were asking him for a king.

It is remarkable to watch the most unlikely people rise to positions of prominence, power and influence. In Czechoslovakia, an enemy of the state has been unanimously elected President by a parliament packed with the people who had thrown him in jail. Newsweek calls Vaclav Havel "the prisoner who took the castle."

Perhaps he is the most improbable leader on the current international political scene. He is a man whose world does not turn on polls, but on principles; not on convenience or career, but on conviction and character. In fact, he was even reluctant to take the job because of his complete lack of experience in governmental affairs. Nonetheless, this poet-playwright has become the most recent symbol of Eastern Europe's rebellion against communism.

How history will judge him and how successful his Presidency will be, will not be determined for many years to come. But one thing is certain, Vaclav Havel, charged with subversion and jailed on three different occasions since 1977, is faced now with the opportunity of a lifetime. And the entire world waits to see what he does with the opportunity he has been given.

Saul was the first king of Israel. At the outset of his career, he seemed to possess all the ingredients necessary for success. But somewhere along the line, things started to go wrong for Saul and his reign ended with his suicide.

When we read about a tragedy like Saul's, it's only natural to want to know why such a thing happened, what went wrong, and if it could have been avoided. So, let's take a closer look at his life and see what happened to this man who forfeited the opportunity of a lifetime.

Let's look first at the opportunity he was given. With all that challenged the people of Israel, it was time for a king who had strength of a single minded devotion to the plan of God.

Saul was the perfect candidate. He had a great deal going for him. He was deeply religious and unquestionably moral. He was modest. He had no political agenda. He did not go after the job, the job sought him.

Physically, he was an impressive man—handsome, and literally head and shoulders taller than the average Hebrew. He was courageous in battle. Saul had a charismatic personality that charmed and inspired other people to do what he wanted them to do.

His story begins with a rather mundane episode involving his father's donkeys. They became lost one day while grazing in the pasture. So, Saul's father, Kish, sent his son and a servant to find the donkeys and bring them home. The two of them looked for three days but could not find them.

On the third day, the servant suggested that they go into the nearby town and see if the local prophet could help them. The prophet, whose name was Samuel told them that the donkeys had been found and that they were already home.

Then, he invited Saul and his servant to stay for a worship service planned later that same day and urged them to even stay through the night. In fact, Samuel told them that a special dinner was already being prepared in Saul's honor.

But the most troubling thing for Saul was what the prophet told him during a private conversation. "You are destined to become the king of Israel," he said. Saul immediately protested, disqualifying himself and altogether declining the opportunity. However, before Saul took his leave of the prophet on the next morning, Samuel privately anointed him king and God uniquely confirmed the action by the outpouring of the His Spirit. With that, it quickly became clear that this opportunity was actually a part of God's plan for Saul's life. It was a call of God, a challenge offered by the One who had created Saul for this task.

It's a remarkable story, don't you agree? A young man goes out to look for his father's lost farm animals and comes back four days later crowned a king. Suddenly, he's yanked out of anonymity and thrown into the public arena where he's expected to unite and lead a nation through one crisis after another. How do you figure it?

Besides, what's all this got to do with you and me? Frankly, it reminds us of the way most opportunities come to us. The day begins like every other day and then, unexpectedly, we come to a turning point, to a fork in the road which leads to what Robert Frost calls "the road less traveled." And when we decide to take that road—if we decide to take that road—it makes all the difference in the world.

Hundreds of years before Saul, another man had stood in shocked belief, his feet rooted to the rocky floor of the desert. He thought he had seen it all, but there was a bush that was burning without being consumed.

He was eighty years old and the last forty of those years he had been a shepherd. His long white beard flapped in the warm breeze. His gnarled hands grasped the shepherd's staff. He had a speech impediment, but now he was being asked to lead millions of people.

"Impossible!" he protested. And, he gave five very good reasons why he couldn't do it. He wasn't the person for the job. He was afraid that people wouldn't understand who had sent him. He was afraid that people wouldn't believe him. He wasn't a good enough speaker to be a leader. And, finally, he just frankly wanted someone else to be sent in his place. Anticipating resistance and rejection from his people, Moses felt that God had used poor judgment in selecting him for such a significant task.

God may not thrust you into the public arena as He did Moses and Saul. He may not give you an assignment as difficult as others who He has called.

Nonetheless, everyday God opens significant doors of opportunity for every one of His children to make a difference. He opens the doors to serve Him and to serve His people.

Listen! You are here because God wants you to be here. Before the foundations of the earth were formed, it was decided that you would be you and you would occupy a particular place, and exercise specific gifts, in such a way as to make a positive difference and a significant impact upon your world.

If you ever see that—and believe that there is a divine purpose for your being here in this place at this time for God's purpose—it will make all the difference in your world. I believe that is the reason for the writer of the text to say, ". . . when he had turned his back to go from Samuel, God gave him another heart." (I Samuel 12:9). It always happens. When you find God's purpose for your life, you become a different person.

I believe that this has taken place in the life of our church. We believe our divine purpose is to worship God and to share His love with all people. That is the hub around which everything revolves concerning the life of our church. Everything we do is an expression of that purpose. That's why committee work is so important because we are planning for the express purpose to worship God and share his love with all people. That's why our PeopleReach program is so important because we are finding people with whom to share God's love. That's why the Sunday School, Church Training, WMU, Brotherhood, Music, Deacon ministry, the Bridgebuilders and all the aspects of our church are important. The purpose of them all is to worship God to share His love with all people. We don't do these things because they are things an organized church does. We do them because that is what pleases God.

If you haven't noticed the change within our church in the last few months, then you need to begin to pay attention. God has given us a new heart. We are different because we have recaptured this purpose. Just like Saul, God has given to us an opportunity make a difference in our world.

Now, let's look at the options available to Saul. Obviously, he could accept or reject the opportunity to serve as Israel's king. But once Saul had been anointed and assumed national leadership, there were other choices which had to be made.

For instance, Saul was free to obey God in every detail or to obey God only when it seemed practical, or otherwise to follow his own inclinations. Shortly after he became king, there was a skirmish between small units of the Israelite army and the Philistines. In response to their rather sound defeat, the Philistines gathered all their forces to stage an invasion of Israel.

Saul rallied his army for a major confrontation. He called Samuel to come and offer a sacrifice to consecrate the effort to God. However, Samuel did not show up when he was expected and Saul sensed the mounting tension with his troops. Poised on the other side of the valley was the entire Philistine army and the Israelites were beginning to defect.

So, like most of us, Saul panicked in what appeared to be a tight spot. Like most of us, he wanted an immediate solution to a significant problem, and he decided to push ahead without God's approval. Saul offered the sacrifice himself. And wouldn't know it, just as the ceremony was ending, Samuel showed up and expressed his outrage that the King had not waited.

Didn't Samuel understand? Under the circumstances, there was nothing else for Saul to do. And frankly, even from our perspective, his action seems excusable—certainly not a major moral offense. So, why make such a big deal about it anyway?

Simply stated, the central issue is that whatever reason Saul had, he did the wrong thing. It revealed that, in a tight spot, Saul was not willing to obey God if it meant waiting on him, or if it he could figure his own way out of the situation. Ant that is why it was such a big deal.

It happens to us all the time. We find ourselves in situations where we must choose between obeying God or doing what seems most practical and expedient. We can tell a little lie and make a profitable deal. We can fail to record all our cash income and with the IRS. They'll probably never find out! We can falsify a few details on our job or credit application and nobody will ever know the difference.

But the irony of the sin of disobedience is this. We may make a huge profit in the short run, but over the long haul it only weakens us and strengthens Satan's hold on our lives. We give Satan permission to take over more and more in our lives.

Saul was a good man. He had everything going for him. But he found himself in a tight spot and he fell. And that's what happens to us when we begin to compromise the will of God in our life.

There is no question that life is difficult, the choices are hard, and our options are not always clear. But the first act of disobedience quickly opens the door to other defiant and sinful acts.

If you read the entire story of Saul, you will discover that no one in the Bible confessed his sin more freely and openly than he. But when you turn the page, you find him doing the same thing again.

Was he insincere in his confession? No more so than are you and I. In fact, one of the greatest frustrations of the Christian experience is the problem of what to do when you've sinned and said, "I'm sorry," but then you go right back and sin again.

What do you do? Saul never discovered how to deal with his tendency toward sin and rebellion. He took one step in the right direction, but he never seemed willing to go any farther. He would become aware of his sin and, without hesitation, admit it. And that's good. The first step toward dealing with sin is to confess it, to own up to it as my sin and to accept full responsibility for it.

But that's not all there is to it. One preacher noticed that hundreds of cars drove by the church every day, but apparently none noticed it. Attendance was declining each Sunday. He called a staff meeting to discuss what might be done. The staff decided to put up a sign right by the busy street. The sign read: "If You're Tired of Sin, Come on In." A few days later, the preacher noticed that someone had scribbled an additional line on the bottom of the sign which said, "But If You're Not, Call 555-1234."

Saul admitted his sin, but apparently what was missing was genuine sorrow about the sin and a willingness to turn loose from it. Because of compromise after compromise, Satan had gained such a hold on Saul's life he was completely incapable of repentance. He knew it was killing him but he couldn't turn loose.

Sam Jones was a famous evangelist. During his evangelistic campaigns he would have what he called a "Quitting Service." He would issue the invitation for people to come forward and confess the sins they were quitting. A man would walk down the aisle and say, "Preacher, I'm a drunk and I am going to quit drinking." Another person would come down the aisle to say, "Preacher, I've been a gossip and I'm going to quit." Sometimes, someone would come down the aisle and confess, "I've been unfaithful to my husband or wife, and I'm going to quit."

Perhaps that's the answer for you: through the convicting power of the Holy Spirit, become aware of you sin. And then, through the grace of God who promises forgiveness and cleansing, you come to simply quit it.

During one of Sam Jones services, a lady came down to the front during the invitation hymn. The pastor asked her what sin she wanted to quit. She answered, "Brother pastor, I ain't been doing nothing and I'm going to quit."

That's the way it is with many other people, perhaps most. You haven't been doing anything and you ought to quit. It's not so much that you've been bad. Rather, it's that you have been good for nothing. You haven't been praying and you need to quit. You haven't been giving and you need to quit.

You haven't been setting a good example and you need to quit. You haven't trusted Christ as your savior and you need to trust him today.

What is it for you? Are you willing to take that step and make the decision to be what God wants you to be and to do what God what you to do. This is the day which God has set before you an opportunity. What will you do? Well . . .

IN THE WINGS

I Samuel 16:1-13

The Lord said to Samuel, "How long will you grieve over Saul? I have rejected him from being king over Israel. Fill your horn with oil and set out; I will send you to Jesse the Bethlehemite, for I have provided for myself a king among his sons." Samuel said, "How can I go? If Saul hears of it, he will kill me." And the Lord said, "Take a heifer with you, and say, 'I have come to sacrifice to the Lord.' Invite Jesse to the sacrifice, and I will sh to meet him trembling, and said, "Do you come peaceably?" He said, "Peaceably; I have come to sacrifice to the Lord; sanctify yourselves and come with me to the sacrifice." And ow you what you shall do; and you shall anoint for me the one whom I name to you." Samuel did what the Lord commanded, and came to Bethlehem. The elders of the city came he sanctified Jesse and his sons and invited them to the sacrifice.

When they came, he looked on Eliab and thought, "Surely the Lord's anointed is now before the Lord." But the Lord said to Samuel, "Do not look on his appearance or on the height of his stature, because I have rejected him; for the Lord does not see as mortals see; they look on the outward appearance, but the Lord looks on the heart." Then Jesse called Abinadab, and made him pass before Samuel. He said, "Neither has the Lord chosen this one." Then Jesse made Shammah pass by. And he said, "Neither has the Lord chosen this one." Jesse made seven of his sons pass before Samuel, and Samuel said to Jesse, "The Lord has not chosen any of these." Samuel said to Jesse, "Are all your sons here?" And he said, "There remains yet the youngest, but he is keeping the sheep." And Samuel said to Jesse, "Send and bring him; for we will not sit down until he comes here." He sent and brought him in. Now he was ruddy, and had beautiful eyes, and was handsome. The Lord said, "Rise and anoint him; for this is the one." Then Samuel took the horn of oil, and anointed him in the presence of his brothers; and the spirit of the Lord came mightily upon David from that day forward. Samuel then set out and went to Ramah.

1809 was a very good year. Of course, nobody knew it at the time because every eye was on Napoleon as he swept across Austria. Little else seemed significant. The dictator of France was the talk of Europe. The terror of his reign made his name synonymous with military superiority and ruthless ambition.

That same year, while war was being waged and history was made, babies were being born in England and America. Seemingly insignificant things were developing while Austria was falling. In 1809 a veritable host of thinkers and statesmen drew their first breaths. William Goldstone was born in Liverpool. Alfred Tennyson began his life in Lincolnshire. Oliver Wendell Holmes made his first cry in Cambridge, Massachusetts. Edgar Allan Poe, in nearby Boston, began his notable life. And in Hodgenville, Kentucky, in a rugged log cabin owned by an illiterate laborer and his wife, were heard the tiny screams of their newborn son, Abraham Lincoln.

All this and more happened in 1809, but nobody noticed. The destiny of the world was being shaped by Napoleon over in Austria, or was it? The "nobodies" nobody noticed were the beginning of a new era. It was there lives, their brains, their writings that would dent the destiny of the entire world.

There was once another year that was a very good year. Saul, the Napoleon of his day, was the king of Israel. Israel's elected king had begun to fissure under the weighty demands of his role. Rashness, compromise and open rebellion against God began to seep in the cracks and saturate his shattered character with sin. Finally, confronted by Samuel, Saul was informed that God had rejected him as king of Israel. Samuel relayed the message from God to Saul:

> Thy kingdom shall not continue. The Lord hath sought him a man after his own heart, and the Lord hath commanded him to be captain over his people, because thou hast not kept that which the Lord commanded thee. (I Samuel 13:14)

The people of Israel focused their attention on Saul while all along God was focusing his attention on someone who was waiting in the wings. A person who would change the course of Israel, forever. He was a young, unassuming shepherd boy named David.

I Samuel 16:1 begins the Biblical account of the life of David. It is an intriguing story of suspense, romance, conflict and scandal. Most of all, it is a story of a imperfect man who struggles to serve a perfect God. Since we are imperfect men and women who still struggle to serve the same perfect God whom David served, what can we learn from the story of David that will help us? How can we avoided the pitfalls that David suffered? How can we attain the victories that David attained in his life?

Let's begin by examining these verses that are written about the beginning of David's reign as king. There are certain truths which we can draw from the facts of this story to apply to our lives.

First of all, when we find our life circumstances cause us to panic, God is already moving and working behind the scenes to bring about his purpose.

All eyes had been on Saul. Now, suddenly, he was stripped of his authority. God had rejected him as Israel's king. The people panicked. It is very possible that the news of Saul's rejection started a national panic. As the word spread from town to town the people felt lost without a leader, a king. To them, no king meant no protection. They had forgotten that God was their protector, their sword and their shield. At the moment of their panic God had already chosen another man for the job.

One would think that the prophet of God, Samuel, would have understood that God was his protector. Even Samuel was unsettled. The fact is, no one is exempt from the feeling of fear. These are the words that the Lord spoke to Samuel:

> How long will you grieve over Saul, since I have rejected him from being King over Israel? Fill you horn with oil, and go; I will send you to Jesse the Bethlehemite, for I have selected a king for Myself among his sons. (I Samuel 16:1)

What causes you to panic? Are you uneasy about what next week holds in store? Are you scared to think about tomorrow? What circumstance in your life are you most uncertain? The songwriter says:

I don't know what the future holds but I know who holds the future. I may listen to a thousand voices but I only hear one whisper.

When Wallace Johnson, builder of numerous Holiday Inn motels and convalescent hospitals, was forty years old, he worked in a sawmill. One morning the boss called him into his office and fired him. Depressed and discouraged, he felt like the world had caved in on him. It was during the depression and he and his wife were in great need of he small wage he had been earning.

He went home and told his wife of his firing and told her he was going to mortgage their little home and go into the construction business.

His first venture was the construction of two small buildings. Within five years he was a multi-millionaire.

"Today, if I could locate the man who fired me," said Mr. Johnson, "I would sincerely thank him for what he did. At the time it happened, I didn't understand why I was fired. Later, I saw that it was unerring and wondrous plan to get me into the way of His choosing!"

When the circumstances of our lives bring us to the verge of panic, don't forget that God is already moving and working to bring about his purpose.

Secondly, while we judge people by looking at their external qualities, God judges people by looking at their inward qualities.

It was not every day that the "preacher" went to someone's town much less to someone's house. They could not figure why Samuel was in town. Samuel assures them of his peaceful intentions and goes about the task that God has sent him to do.

One by one the sons of Jesse passed in front of Samuel. Eliab gets Samuel's attention. He's tall and probably good looking. He has all the external qualities that a king should have. Quickly, God tells Samuel to keep looking. He says:

> Do not look on his countenance or the height of his stature, because I have refused him; for the Lord seeth not as man seeth; for man looketh on the outward appearance, but the Lord looketh upon the heart. (I Samuel 16:7)

Finally the parade of sons came to an end and no King was found. Each of the sons looked liked a king, but in God's book externals don't carry a great deal of weight. After all, Saul looked like a king. If Samuel received his signals correctly, God had refused each of them.

Chris wanted to play college basketball more than anything else, yet, he was barely 6 feet tall. He was a no-name, a retread, too young even though he was out of High School. To complicate things even further, he suffers from a disease called Tourette Syndrome which is a disorder affecting his nervous system. He had no external qualities that a college basketball player should have, except one . . . he was the best player that ever came out of Gulfport High in Gulfport, Mississippi.

Dale Brown from Louisiana State University, spotted him on a recruiting trip. He saw his potential and gave him a scholarship to play with the Bengal Tigers. He is in the middle of his freshman year at LSU and has scored 50 points in three different games. His name is Chris Jackson.

Even though he has no external qualities of a basketball player, he has the inward drive that produces result.

David was like that. He did not look like a king, he was a no-name, a retread, to young for the job. God's choice is always based on the rock solid qualities of the heart. God does not measure character by external appearance or personal charisma. His chief criterion is: "Are you willing to do My will?"

Vance Havner once said, "Don't pray that God will use you, but pray that God will make you usable!" Isn't it true that many times you and I are more interested in receiving the recognition of our service rather than having that inner sense that are hearts are prepared for God's use? David's character was built by the clay and brick of faithfulness in the little things, the unseen, the unknown, the unappreciated, and the unapplauded. Yet because of David's faithfulness in the little things God saw, God knew, God appreciated, and God applauded.

Thirdly, while we overlook the insignificant, God notices the insignificant. It is in the little things that we prove ourselves capable of the big things. Before entrusting David with the lives of the entire nation of Israel, God first gave him a flock of sheep to protect.

So the seven men were seated, apparently these were all of the sons of Jesse. Since God had promised a king from among Jesse's sons, Samuel was sure that there was another. Samuel asks, "Are these all of your children? With an "oh-yeah-I-almost-forgot" reply Jesse reveals that there is one who is keeping the sheep, David. In Jesse's way of thinking, the youngest son was insignificant. He was the least. He was unimportant. What could he contribute? Then Samuel said to Jesse:

"Send and fetch him; for we will not sit down until he comes here. And he sent, and brought him in. Now he was a ruddy, and of a beautiful, and handsome. And the Lord said, Arise, anoint him; for this is he. (I Samuel 16:11-12)

David's life was never the same. As the oil ran down his freckled face, something else was taking place. The spirit of God came upon him. To give him the strength, the power and the humility that would be characteristics of the great king of Israel.

F.B. Meyer describes the day of David's anointing:

It began like any ordinary day. No angel trumpet heralded it. No faces looked out of the heaven. The sun arose that morning according to his wont over the purple walls of the hills of Moab, making the cloud-curtains saffron and gold. With the first glimmer of light the boy was on his way to lead his flock to pasture-lands heavy with dew. As the morning hours sped onwards, many duties would engross his watching soul—strengthening the weak, healing that which was sick, binding up that which was broken, and seeking that which was lost; or the music of his song may have filled the listening air.

Today is like any other day . . . or is it? It seems to be a routine, ordinary, unassuming Sunday morning. It is just the kind of morning God chooses the lowly ones, the insignificant to rule His kingdom . . . or the kind of day that he calls you to step from the wings and accept the unexpected grace that He has for you.

FOR CAVE DWELLERS ONLY

David left there and escaped to the cave of Adullam; when his brothers and all his father's house heard of it, they went down there to him.

Few historical events paint a picture as black and bitter as those that surrounded the Nazi regime. As Hitler persecuted and tortured, millions of people were mercilessly killed. Yet, during those years of abysmal darkness, the light of protection and security flickered through. On the top floor of a crooked little Dutch house, Corrie ten Boom and her family built a secret room to provide a hiding place for many of those hunted people.

Over a period of time hundreds of Jews passed to safety through the walls of the ten Boom's home. Once the Gestapo discovered their secret, Corrie was torn from her comfortable home in Haarlem and locked in a dank prison cell in Schevenigan.

Once a provider of safety, Corrie herself now needed a hiding place. Although no such place was to be found in the prisons and concentration camps she sheltered herself in the Lord.

David also suffered undeserved persecution. Fleeing from Saul's angry sword, he sought a hiding place in a dark, damp cave in Adullam. While in hiding, David reached one of the lowest and most desperate points of his life. He also discovered the light of God's deliverance. While his body was hiding in a cave, his soul was hidden in the clefts of God's granite love.

Do you find yourself in a cave trying to find refuge in God? Is there a place where you can turn where your soul finds contentment and satisfaction? How can we find the light of God's deliverance while facing low and desperate times in our life?

Psalm 142 was written by David while he was in the cave at Adullam. The Psalms are like an entry into David's diary. Here we can glimpse into the feelings of David and draw truths from his experience with God that will help us when we discover we are in the low and desperate points of life.

David was characterized as being a man after God's own heart. He desired for God to have His way with him. Yet, David found himself in a cave desperately needing protection from his enemies. Perhaps we could call him a caveman after God's own heart! If we are to have the success that he had when he found himself desperate we must totally depend on God's way for our life. If we are not committed to God's way for our life our desperation could turn into destruction.

We will not escape despair because we are people after God's own heart. It does not mean that we will necessarily be removed from our cave of despair. It does mean that the cave can be transformed and transfigured. It means our life may not continue in the same manner but it can still be good.

One of the great fallacies of modern day Christianity is that because we have faith in God we will not suffer. We seem to equivocate faith in God with painless living.

Let me share with you a bit of wisdom of my father. He used to say he would rather a loaf of bread costing a dollar and have the dollar to buy it than to have the same loaf of bread costing a nickel and not have the nickel. I think this can be applied to living with God.

I would rather have great pain and a relationship with God than to have little pain and no relationship with God.

There is a Chinese parable which tells of an old woman who had lost her son. She was so grief stricken that she did nothing except stand before a wailing wall in her home and grieve.

One day a Chinese philosopher saw the woman in her distress. He told the woman to bring him a mustard seed from the home in China that had never experienced sorrow and he would bring her son back to life.

So, she searched throughout all of China. She traveled to every hamlet, every village, every town. Still she was unable to find a home in which sorrow had not come. Realizing her selfishness she returned to the old philosopher and said, "How selfish I have been with my grief, sorrow is common to all."

We are never left alone if we are people after God's own heart.

> I cried unto the Lord with my voice; with my voice unto the Lord did I make my supplication. I poured out my complaint before him; I showed him my trouble. (Psalm 142:1-2)

Although David had to forsake his position, family, mentor and friend he did not have to forsake God. God was still there in the cave to hear his complaint.

Once a little girl was asked, "Why is there just one God?" She thought and said, "Because God fills every place and there's's no room for another."

We must remember that the same God who leads us in good times will also lead through the bad ones. The same God who is with us during the mountain experiences is with us during the valley of our life. The same God who is with us in the daytime is with us in the dark night of our soul.

One of the great freethinkers of England was Anthony Collins. He was a great orator and debater. He had a brilliant mind.

As he was walking one morning he passed a poor man going in the opposite direction. Mr. Collins said to the man, "Where are you going?" "To church to worship God," replied the old man. "Tell me," said Collins hoping to embarrass the man, "Is your God a great God or a small God?"

After much thought the old man responded, "My God is so great that the Heavens of Heaven cannot contain him. He is so small that he may dwell within my heart."

God was with David in the cave. God is with us in our times of desperation.

We can find purpose and direction if we are people after God's own heart.

> When my spirit was overwhelmed within me, then thou knewest
> my path. (Psalm 142:3)

Even though David was not sure which way to go, God did. When he was down and out and desperate he could say with confidence that God knew his path.

Much research has been about the glowworm. It has been observed that the little worm traveled at a pace that was not easily detected by human observance. After years of study it has been determined that the worm would only go as far as its light would shine.

David said in another Psalm that God's word was "a lamp unto his feet." We can depend upon God to give us the direction for our daily living.

We can find our portion if we are people after God's own heart.

> I cried unto the Lord, thou art my refuge and my portion in the
> land of the living. (Psalm 142:5)

David discovered that his resources would fail. His position was not available any longer. His friend could not be there for him as he would have liked. He knew God would not fail him.

God provides all we need. Everything at God's disposal is ours for the asking. It is like saying that a guardian of a well will die of thirst or a fish will die of thirst as it swims in the ocean. It is like saying a mouse will die of starvation in the grain elevators of Kansas or an eagle will suffocate as it soars in the air above. God will take care of His own. God will take care of you. We can bear great burdens with greater fortitude when we can see the beacon of God's care.

God will deal bountifully with us again if we are people after his own heart.

> Bring my soul out of prison, that I may praise thy name: righteous
> shall compass me about; for thou shalt deal bountifully with me.
> (Psalm 142:7)

Like David, whose songs reverberated a message of faith and hope within the cave's rocky walls, we can sing songs that attest to our hope in God.

Most likely, you and I will never have to seek refuge from the cruelty of a concentration camp or the sword of an angry king. But as God's child, we have enemies all around from whom you will need to flee—temptations, weaknesses, people who trample your faith. When you face an enemy remember that God has a hiding place for you, a place of protection, comfort, and direction for your life. There he will put a song of deliverance in your heart.

> You are my hiding place
> You shelter me from the snares of my enemies
> and surround me with
> sweet songs of deliverance that
> balm the bitter wounds
> of my despair
> I will trust in You, O Lord, yes
> I will trust in You
> For there in your safe and secret place
> You will sing over my broken spirit
> And You will make me whole.

THE GIFT THAT SOOTHES

I Samuel 16:14-23

Now the spirit of the Lord departed from Saul, and an evil spirit from the Lord tormented him. And Saul's servants said to him, "See now, an evil spirit from God is tormenting you. Let our lord now command the servants who attend you to look for someone who is skillful in playing the lyre; and when the evil spirit from God is upon you, he will play it, and you will feel better." So Saul said to his servants, "Provide for me someone who can play well, and bring him to me." One of the young men answered, "I have seen a son of Jesse the Bethlehemite who is skillful in playing, a man of valor, a warrior, prudent in speech, and a man of good presence; and the Lord is with him." So Saul sent messengers to Jesse, and said, "Send me your son David who is with the sheep." Jesse took a donkey loaded with bread, a skin of wine, and a kid, and sent them by his son David to Saul. And David came to Saul, and entered his service. Saul loved him greatly, and he became his armor-bearer. Saul sent to Jesse, saying, "Let David remain in my service, for he has found favor in my sight." And whenever the evil spirit from God came upon Saul, David took the lyre and played it with his hand, and Saul would be relieved and feel better, and the evil spirit would depart from him.

George Bernard Shaw once put up a monument in the church yard at Windlesham in Surrey, England, in memory of Clara and Henry Higgs. They were the couple who had faithfully worked for Mr. Shaw for many years. They would tend the garden and the house, setting him free to work as a dramatist and playwright. No one has been serve better. Clara and Henry Higgs belong to a great army of people who never do anything big or famous themselves, but whose service is indispensable to others.

The same might be said of a young shepherd boy in the palace of a King, playing his harp and singing his tunes to soothe a ruthless and unsettled king.

The political and spiritual climates of Israel were shaky at best. The palace staff did not know what to do. The king had been rejected by God and it had severe emotional effects on Saul. The people were unsettled and insecure. What would their future hold for them? Who would be there knew king? Was their kingdom coming to an end?

Saul had lived a life of open rebellion against the God of his people. Many times he had taken matters into his own hands and had blown it. Now he was feeling the effects of the guilty conscience caused by his own disobedience to what he believed to be the will of God and his consequent break with Samuel, the man who was instrumental in bringing him the throne. This bad conscience robbed Saul of self-confidence and his sense of the presence of God.

On a recent Barbara Walters Special, Johnny Cash told in an interview the unbelievable story of his early adult life. He detailed his problems with drugs and alcohol. He also described the years he spent in prison because of crimes he had committed. Johnny testifies that if it was not for Jesus Christ and the faith that he has placed in Christ that life would not be worth anything to him today. He says the presence of God in his life is the most important part of his life. As the closing questions, Barbara Walters asks, "When you die, will you go to Heaven or Hell?" His response was poignant. "Heaven, because I have already experienced Hell."

The point is this—without a sense of the presence of God in one's life, there is no hope, no peace, no assurance, no life. It is like Hell.

Saul was alone. Desperate and depressed. Guilty. Saul's servants knew that he needed help. Where could they turn? They said:

> Let our lord now command thy servants, who are before thee, to seek out a man, who is a skillful player on a harp; and it shall come to pass, when the evil spirit from God is upon thee, that he shall play with his hand, and thou shalt be well. (I Samuel 16:16)

The story of David in the courts of Saul has some important lessons for us to heed concerning the small deeds we do for others. Think of the receptionists and flower arrangers and committee members who do their work without acknowledgment or publicity; the cooks and the servers and ushers and teachers who work unselfishly from month to month to make things go, to fill in the gaps, to see that the kingdom marches on. It isn't the ten-talent people that heaven will belong to; it's the one- or two-talent people who gladly use their talents for God. They are the ones who hold everything together and make it work. They are the unsung heroes.

First—God sometimes uses the least of our talents to help others. All of our talents must be a God's disposal.

The servants had someone in mind for the job of playing for Saul. His qualifications were:

> He is skillful in playing, and a mighty, valiant man, and a man of
> war, and prudent in matters, and an agreeable person, and the Lord
> is with Him. (I Samuel 16:18)

That's not a bad resume'. At this point and time, it was the least of David's "kingly" qualities that God was wanting to use.

Kenneth Lundberg, who lives in Riverside, Rhode Island, works at a nearby university. Every day, Kenneth walks from his car to his office through a twenty-foot stretch of lawn.

For a long time, the lawn annoyed him because it was littered with can, papers, and other debris thrown down by students. He thought of writing letters to the editor of the school paper, and even of organizing a clean-up day; but he decided that nothing would be done and he would only succeed in raising his blood pressure.

Then one day Kenneth got an idea. He would take ownership of the plot of ground. He didn't tell anyone about this, as it was probably against some regulation or other. But he made himself personally responsible for the environment quality of this twenty-foot piece of lawn.

Each day, going to and from his car, Kenneth picked up the litter. He made a game of it, limiting himself to ten items each way. At first he carried it to a wastebasket in the building or took it to the car and carried it home with him. Then a curious thing occurred: large orange barrels appeared at each end of the lawn. Someone on the maintenance crew was his silent conspirator.

Finally Kenneth reached the point where he was picking faster than other people were littering. He looked with pride at his twenty-foot lawn. It was beautifully green and free of trash. The rest of the campus was as littered as ever. But that was someone else's problem. He was taking care of his.

Kenneth has been tending his lawn for years now, and his one-minute walk through it on his way to and from work is the highlight of his day. He begins and ends his workday in a positive mood. He uses the least of his qualifications to perform a task that he feels he must do.

What gift are you keeping to yourself? Do you only look for great and grandiose things to do while little things go undone? How often has your life been sweetened and sustained by the little acts of human kindness performed by people whose names will never go down in history for deeds done?

Second—God wants us to serve others unselfishly. To this point in the story, David has yet to utter a word. In the stories of other great men of the Old Testament one quickly hears so-called reasons why they are not the right person for the task. This element is absent in the beginning of David's story. Note David's response to the task:

> Jesse took an ass laden with bread, and a skin of wine, and a kid, and sent them by David, his son, unto Saul. And David came to Saul, and stood before him; and he loved him greatly; and he became his armor bearer. (I Samuel 16:20-21)

Recently I spoke with a former pastor of First Baptist Church of Memphis, Tennessee. In our conversation he began talking about his love for the pastorate. He said he enjoyed all aspects of being a pastor except for the aspect related to the work of the nominating committee. He assumed that anyone should be willing to serve the church. It seemed to him that one should not have to be begged into service.

David did not have to begged into service. He willingly accepted the role. Like David, we should be willing to serve. We do not know how what we say or do will affect others.

Jake and Harry were big fishing buddies. One day as they were fishing Harry took his teeth out and laid them on the seat behind him in the boat. Jim saw this as an opportunity to "get" Harry, so Jim replaced Harry's teeth with his teeth and placed Harry's teeth in his pocket. After some minutes passed, Harry reached for what he thought was his teeth and put them back in his mouth. Aggravated because they did not fit well, he exclaimed,

"These things never have fit well!" and threw them in the lake.

Jake did not know what to do. All he could think of was his well-fit teeth, for which he had paid good money, sinking to the bottom of the lake never to be worn again. After some quick thinking, Jake removed Harry's teeth from his pocket and declared, "My teeth have never fit either!" and threw them into the water.

Third—God can use seemingly insignificant efforts to give meaning to the lives of others. David's effort to sooth Saul worked.

> . . . David took an harp, and played with his hand; so Saul was refreshed, and was well, and the evil spirit departed from him. (I Samuel 16:23)

In Dostoevsky's *The Brothers Karamazov* there is a moving illustration of this. Dimitri had been sentenced to prison in Siberia. He is so exhausted that he falls asleep on a bench, and, when he awakens, he finds that someone has placed a pillow under his head.

He doesn't know who has done it, but he is elated. It is a sign of the goodness of life. He will go to prison, he says, and keep God's name alive there, because he knows that God is in the world. The nameless, selfless act of someone who did him an insignificant kindness is guarantee of that.

Fourth—It is in giving of ourselves in service to others that we serve the Lord.

Brother Lawrence, the author of *The Practice of the Presence of God*, found that worshiping God meant much more than being in a certain place at a certain time of the week. He discovered that worship should occur wherever our life leads us. We can worship God as we wash pots and pans, or sweep the floor. We must take what we learn in this holy place and apply it in the market place.

Have you given God access to all of your life? What about the seemingly insignificant talents that you have. Are you waiting for a ten-talent opportunity while God asks you to do a one-talent task? Let us commit our small talents as well as our large ones so that God can be served in a better way.

FACING INTIMIDATION

I Samuel 17

Now the Philistines gathered their armies for battle; they were gathered at Socoh, which belongs to Judah, and encamped between Socoh and Azekah, in Ephes-dammim. Saul and the Israelites gathered and encamped in the valley of Elah, and formed ranks against the Philistines. The Philistines stood on the mountain on one side, and Israel stood on the mountain on the other side, with a valley between them. And there came out from the camp of the Philistines a champion named Goliath, of Gath, whose height was six cubits and a span. He had a helmet of bronze on his head, and he was armoured with a coat of mail; the weight of the coat was five thousand shekels of bronze. He had greaves of bronze on his legs and a javelin of bronze slung between his shoulders. The shaft of his spear was like a weaver's beam, and his spear's head weighed six hundred shekels of iron; and his shield-bearer went before him. He stood and shouted to the ranks of Israel, 'Why have you come out to draw up for battle? Am I not a Philistine, and are you not servants of Saul? Choose a man for yourselves, and let him come down to me. If he is able to fight with me and kill me, then we will be your servants; but if I prevail against him and kill him, then you shall be our servants and serve us.' And the Philistine said, 'Today I defy the ranks of Israel! Give me a man, that we may fight together.' When Saul and all Israel heard these words of the Philistine, they were dismayed and greatly afraid.

In 1501, an unformed block of crudely cut marble lay untouched in a cathedral workshop in Italy. By the beginning of 1504, Michelangelo had transformed it into his largest sculpture as it still stands today in Florence's Galleria dell' Academia. It is the statue of David. Frederick Hart describes the statue like this:

> It has all the passionate drama of man's inner nature. The sinews of the neck seem to tense and relax, the veins of the neck, hands, and wrist seem to fill, the nostrils flair, the belly muscles contracts and the chest lifts with the intake of breath, the whole proud being quivers like a war horse that smells the battle. But of the nature of the battle there is no indication.

Indeed, in the statue, Michelangelo has made stone to breathe. Chiseled into the giant sculpture are some of the qualities that marked David as a man of God. It displays his solid-marble strength, his colossal character, his larger-than-life faith. It is symbolic in nature of what God did in the life of the shepherd boy. The unformed, unpolished young adolescent was transformed into the mighty King of Israel. He was transformed because his heart was soft and maluable and tuned to the will of God. Even the slingshot slung over his shoulder symbolizes not action but attribute. In battle the young warrior relied not upon his meager material resources but upon the abundant power of the Lord.

Today we want to take another look at the story of David and Goliath. Let's examine what took place that day on the battlefield. Let's see who the giant really was. Let's apply the truths of the story to our lives today.

Picture a vast canyon enclosed by mountains on both sides, the Philistines on one side and the Israelites on the other. They were like blankets of humanity thrown across the mountain's shoulders. On this particular day the battle was not to be between two armies, but between two representatives, one from each side of the valley.

Enter Goliath of Gath. He was an enormous bully. All nine and a half feet of him was fully enclosed with armor. He was not only huge, he appeared impenetrable, his appearance was intimidating.

His appearance was not his only intimidating feature. His words were merciless. He said:

> Why do you come out to draw up in battle array? Am I not the Philistine and you servants of Saul? Choose a man yourselves and let him come down to me. If he is able to fight with me and kill me, then we will become your servants; but if I prevail, then you shall become our servants and serve us. (I Samuel 17:8-9)

Goliath's taunting was relentless. He gave his challenge, not just once, but twice a day for forty days. The Israelites were facing what appeared to be an intimidating and hopeless circumstance.

We have problems and troubles that attack us daily. Whether they are people, pressures, worries, or fears they consistently taunt us. Sometimes they are no more than a slight nuisance. Yet, at other times the challenge they present shakes and rattles the foundation of our hearts. What is your response when you face situations that seem hopeless? How do you react? How can we live with these intimidations and echo David's song:

> I love Thee, O Lord, My strength. The Lord is my rock and my fortress and my deliverer, My God, my rock, in whom I take refuge; My shield and the horn of my salvation, my stronghold. I call upon the Lord, who is worthy to be praised, and I saved from my enemies. (Psalm 18:1-3)

Let's glean some practical applications from what happens in this story so that we can better handle intimidating circumstances in our own lives.

First—When we face intimidating circumstances, we must not become paralyzed by our fear. We control fear or fear controls us. When we control fear it can work to our advantage. When we allow our fear to control us it cause the intimidation to increase.

Saul was neglecting his responsibility to fight Goliath. He was dismayed and afraid. He was controlled by his fear. He wanted someone else to fight the battle. The reward for fighting the battle would include financial gain, Saul's daughter and freedom from taxation. No one seemed interested in his offer.

Enter an unassuming shepherd boy, David. He was delivering the items his father had sent to his brothers. Naturally, he was curious about the battle. When he heard the verbiage of the Philistine, David took offense at the insults that had been hurled at the armies of the Living God. His youthful idealism urged him to action. He controlled his fear and used it to his advantage.

It is reported that newspaper counselor, Ann Landers, receives approximately 10,000 letters a month, and nearly all are from people who are burdened with problems. She was asked if any one problem was more predominate than the others. Her reply was that the one problem above all others seemed to be fear. People are afraid of losing their health and wealth, their loved ones. People are afraid of life itself.

The *Prairie Overcomer* states it this way. "There are four great impelling motives that move men to action: Fear, hope, faith and love—these four, but the greatest of these is fear. Fear is the first in order, first in force, first in fruit. Indeed, fear is the beginning of wisdom."

Second—When we face intimidating circumstances, we must not forget the lion and the bear. We should remember God`s faithfulness in the past and build our present life upon it.

When David arrived on the scene he began to understand that it was no accident that he had come to visit his brothers that day. He remembered his experience of protecting his father's flock of sheep, Now he had an opportunity to protect the flock of God. He didn't forget the lions and the bears.

We see here the practical results of the loss of the sense of God's presence. Saul, too, had experiences from his past that could have strengthened him for the battle with Goliath.

There was Jonathan who was compared to Michmash because of his fighting ability and then there was Abner, the commander in chief, who made no move to find a brawny young soldier to face the challenge. When David arrives he says these words to Saul:

> Thy servant kept his father's sheep, and there came a lion and a bear, and took a lamb out of the flock; And I went out after him and delivered it out of his mouth. And when he arose against me, I caught him by his beard, and smote him, and slew him. (I Samuel 17:34-35)

Christian leadership does not depend on past successes and failures but how we use them to constantly develop our faith for the challenges of the present and the future.

How easy it is to forget the great hand of God as he has lead us in days gone by. Can you remember a time when God was not faithful to you? Has God ever let you down? Granted there are times when we do not agree with the purpose of God in the events of our lives, but we must trust that the God who has been faithful to us in the past will be faithful to us in the future.

Before the days of modern navigational aids a traveller crossed the Atlantic Ocean in a boat equipped with two compasses. One was fixed to the deck where the man at the wheel could see it. The other compass was fastened on one of the masts, and often a sailor would be seen climbing up to inspect it.

A passenger asked the captain, "Why do you have two compasses?" "This is an iron vessel," replied the captain, "and the compass on the deck is often affected by its surroundings. Such is not the case with the compass at the masthead; that one is above the influence of its surroundings. We steer by the compass above."

Saul was influenced by his surroundings. David was influenced by the leadership of God. It is my observation that one of the reasons many people are bewildered by their life circumstances is that they have not allowed their sense of direction to be influenced by their faith in God, the higher compass. We must fixed our sight on God and His unchanging leadership in our lives.

We ought not to be unmindful of the way by which the Lord our God has led us, for if we are unmindful we shall lose much. Some people have very short memories. It has been well said that we write our benefits in dust and our injuries in marble, and it is equally true that we generally inscribe our affliction upon brass, while we write our deliverances of God on water. It ought not be so. If our memories we are more accurate of the merciful visit of our God, our faith would often be strengthened in times of trial. What did David remember? We must remember the same.

Third—When we face intimidating circumstances, we must not compromise who we are in order to fight the battle by using the tactics of others.

David has approached Saul and he agreed to allow David to fight the Giant under one condition, David was to wear Saul armor.

> Saul armored David with his armor, and put an helmet of bronze upon his head; also he armed him with a coat of mail. And David girded his sword upon his armor, and he attempted to go. (I Samuel 17:38-39)

Picture this, an adolescent boy in the armor of a man who was "head and shoulders" above all the people of Israel. Chuck Swindoll calls it a "36 regular in a 52 long". David attempts to do it Saul's way but realizes he must do it his way if he is to succeed.

It is a great temptation to surrender to the pressures of others and fight with tactics that are not true to who you are as a person. Stories upon stories can be told of persons who have "jumped ship" and gone in a direction contrary to their better judgment. There is the executive who decides to receive some extra cash for some "under the table" favors. There is the college president who decides to fight a battle by the standards of a board of trustees that contrary to his own. There is the teenager who caves into peer pressures and begins to practice things that are against their better judgment. The list goes on and on. George Bernard Shaw puts it aptly:

> If you do things merely because you think some other fool expects you to do them, and he expects you to do them because he thinks you expect him to expect you to do them, it will end in every body doing what nobody wants to do, which is in my opinion a silly state of things.

Fourth—When we face intimidating circumstances, we must rely on the abundant power of God and not on our meager resources.

Most people on the battlefield that day only saw one thing—Goliath. They knew that the odds were against them. When David looked upon that battlefield he saw more than Goliath, he saw the Lord. God was as real to David as Goliath was to the Israelites. David depended upon God's power rather then his meager resources. He says:

> All the earth may know that there is a God of Israel, and that all this assembly may know that the Lord does deliver by sword or by spear; for the battle is the Lord's and He will give you into our hands. (I Samuel 17-46-47)

What about you? Do you depend upon God's power in your life? Or do you depend on your meager resources to fight the battle of faith? God honors those who allow Him to fight their battles.

Fifth—When we face intimidating circumstances, the battle can be won.

> And David put his hand in his bag, and took from there a stone, and slung it, and smote the Philistine in his forehead, that the stone sank into his forehead . . . and David prevailed and cut off his head. (I Samuel 17:49-51)

While Michelangelo's statue was still a huge chunk of stone, it earned the name "the giant." The sculpture may be larger than life but it is true to life of the giant character, devotion, and faith God chiseled in David's soul.

As we face intimidating moments in our life I pray these words of Michelangelo will ring true for us:

> Lord, in the extreme hours, Extend to me Thy pitying arms, take me from myself and make of me one to please Thee.

AFTERMATH OF A GIANT KILLING

I Samuel 17:55-18:16

When Saul saw David go out against the Philistine, he said to Abner, the commander of the army, "Abner, whose son is this young man?" Abner said, "As your soul lives, O king, I do not know." The king said, "Inquire whose son the stripling is." On David's return from killing the Philistine, Abner took him and brought him before Saul, with the head of the Philistine in his hand. Saul said to him, "Whose son are you, young man?" And David answered, "I am the son of your servant Jesse the Bethlehemite."

When David had finished speaking to Saul, the soul of Jonathan was bound to the soul of David, and Jonathan loved him as his own soul. Saul took him that day and would not let him return to his father's house. Then Jonathan made a covenant with David, because he loved him as his own soul. Jonathan stripped himself of the robe that he was wearing, and gave it to David, and his armor, and even his sword and his bow and his belt. David went out and was successful wherever Saul sent him; as a result, Saul set him over the army. And all the people, even the servants of Saul, approved.

As they were coming home, when David returned from killing the Philistine, the women came out of all the towns of Israel, singing and dancing, to meet King Saul, with tambourines, with songs of joy, and with musical instruments. And the women sang to one another as they made merry, "Saul has killed his thousands, and David his ten thousands." Saul was very angry, for this saying displeased him. He said, "They have ascribed to David ten thousands, and to me they have ascribed thousands; what more can he have but the kingdom?" So Saul eyed David from that day on. The next day an evil spirit from God rushed upon Saul, and he raved within his house, while David was playing the lyre, as he did day by day. Saul had his spear in his hand; and Saul threw the spear, for he thought, "I will pin David to the wall." But David eluded him twice.

Saul was afraid of David, because the Lord was with him but had departed from Saul. So Saul removed him from his presence, and made him a commander of a thousand; and David marched out and came in, leading the army. David had success in all his undertakings; for the Lord was with him. When Saul saw that he had great success, he stood in awe of him. But all Israel and Judah loved David; for it was he who marched out and came in leading them.

They were down but not out. The scene appeared hopeless. They had one more man to try it, in order to win the game. His name, Kirk Gibson.

It was in the 1988 World Series in the bottom of the ninth inning with two outs. If he couldn't do it, the Oakland Athletics would win the World Series. If he could do it, his team, the Los Angeles Dodgers, would even the series at 3 games to 3.

To add suspense to the game, Kirk Gibson had two bad knees and had not played in the 6th game for that reason. When Tommy LaSorda weighed the situation he decided to take that big chance and put Gibson in as pinch hitter.

Pitch one. Strike. Pitch two. Ball. Finally the count was 3 and 2, one more pitch at which to swing. The crowd took a collective sigh as the pitcher hurled the baseball to the plate. Gibson swung. He made contact. Foul Ball! Still 3 to 2. Again the pitcher wound to pitch. The ball whizzed toward the plate. Gibson swings and . . . hits the game winning home run. The Dodgers extended the series to the seventh game of the World Series.

The Israelite army were in the bottom of the ninth with two outs and a full count. It looked as if the Philistines would win the battle and make the Israelites their slaves. They were down but not out. They had one more remote shot at a victory. They placed their hopes and dreams in David, Jesse's youngest son, the youthful shepherd boy from Bethlehem who slew lions and bears. He knew the Lord was on His side and would fight his battles for him. The soldiers couldn't believe their eyes when the giant tumbled to the ground. They cheered in amazement as David drew Goliath's sword from its sheath and cut off the giants head. Now, David could add giant slaying to his list of accomplishments. He could remember the lion and the bear and now Goliath. The slaughter of Goliath was only the beginning of the remarkable victories that David would have in his life.

David was a man of glorious triumph and of great tragedy. He was uniquely gifted but human to the core. He was strong in battle but weak at home. David was not a polished personality. He is blood and bone and breath, sharing our struggles of spirit and soul, shaped by the same influences that shape you and me today. What tools did God use to shape David's character? How did he become who God wanted him to be? How are the same things instrumental in developing people today to being people after God's own heart? What is God using to shape and to mold the rock solid qualities of faith that he wants each of us to have?

First of all, God develops our character through those who guide us. The ones who teach us the fundamentals of life are used by God to mold and to shape our being.

Perhaps no one is more influential in the shaping of David's character than his father. David is clearly identified as the son of Jesse the Bethlehemite. What an extraordinary man Jesse the Bethlehemite must have been.

As Saul sees the skill of David as he battles Goliath, he asks Abner to identify who David's father is. Saul says:

> Abner, whose son is this youth? Inquire whose son this stripling
> is. (I Samuel 17:56)

We know from earlier accounts that Saul already knew David's father's name. Here Saul is asking more. He wants to know who taught the stripling the skills of which he displayed. He wanted to know about the heritage of David.

Who in your life gave you the guidance that you needed? Was it a parent, a grandparent, aunt or uncle, or maybe a teacher, who gave you that much needed guidance? There could have been several people who took the time to teach you the fundamentals of living.

In sports, whether it be basketball, football or baseball, fundamentals are a necessity. One cannot advance in expertise until the fundamentals are mastered. When the fundamentals are mastered then the player can move on to higher degrees of difficulty.

Many times after a loss, coaches in every sport have said, "We're going to have to go back to the basics." When a person or a team forgets the basics of their game, defeat is inevitable. The same is true in living. When our priorities become scrambled and find that everything is upside down, it may be time to go back to basics and re-learn the fundamentals.

No one taught me more about the fundamentals of living than my parents. In both word and deed they taught me the essentials in becoming a well rounded person.

Living on a farm brought many opportunities for teaching. At a very young age I learned I had to work. My father would say, "If you are going to eat your going to work." As I grew older into teenage years I learned that I was to follow my parent's rules. "As long as you live under this roof you're going to live by these rules."

I suppose the basic truth I learned while at home, which still steers my life, is that we represent more than ourselves. My daddy would say, "Don't let your name down."

Who has given you guidance? Who is responsible for your being who you are? God develops our character by those who guide us.

Second—God develops our character through those who befriend us. The ones who take us under their wings as friends are being use by God to give us the support we need to go through difficult times.

David's life was marked early on by difficulty. He was fortunate in that he had a friend in Saul's son, Jonathan. Jonathan was the heir apparent to the throne yet he did not react to David's victory with jealousy. In fact, in a grand symbolic jester, Jonathan, gave David his right to the throne.

Jonathan stripped himself of the robe that was upon him, and gave it to David, and his garments, even his sword, and his bow and his belt. (I Samuel 18:4)

Jonathan was a "true blue" friend to David. He stuck by his side through thick and thin. As an old Russian proverb says, "An old friend is better than two new ones." A close friend makes the valleys of our live seem less vast, less threatening, less ominous.

A modern day story of friendship is that of Helen Keller and Anne Sullivan. Helen was born and lived without sight and sound. Anne Sullivan was born in Feeding Hills, Massachusetts. She was born half-blind. When she was a small child her mother died and Anne spent the rest of her childhood in the poorhouse.

The Perkins Institute developed a technique that was very promising to people who were blind. Anne Sullivan was one of their patients. After surgery and treatment Anne received her sight and dedicated her life to help others who were sightless.

Meanwhile, Helen Keller was born in the south. Anne took Helen under her care as one of her students. After a short period of time she had taught Helen 30 words in sign language. Helen Keller rose to renown.

Although they were teacher and pupil, they became great friends. In later life, Anne Sullivan fell upon hard times. She became blind. The student became teacher. Helen taught and cared for Anne until her death.

> I love you not only for what you are, but for what I am with you.
> I love you not only for what you have made yourself, but for what
> you are making of me; I love you for closing your ears to the discord
> in me and for adding to the music in me by worshipful listening;
> You have done it by being yourself. Perhaps that is what being a
> friend means, after all.

How fortunate each of us are to have a close friend to share our sorrows and joys in our life.

Third—God develops our character through those who affirm us.

> David was accepted in the sight of all the people, and also in the
> sight of Saul's servants . . . the women came out of all cities a singing
> and dancing . . . and said, "Saul has killed his thousands and David
> has killed his ten thousands. (I Samuel 18:5-7)

We are all motivated by different things. Some by intimidation and others by encouragement.

Bobby Dodd, a former athletic director of Georgia Tech, tells a story about motivation.

A team he was coaching was leading in the game by a score of 7 to 6. He gave his quarterback strict orders to run the clock out and not to pass the football.

In the last minute of the game the team inched their way down the field. Finally they were on the 10 yard line with only a few seconds left to go in the game. The quarterback could not resist temptation any longer. He wanted a 14 to 6 victory rather than a 7 to 6 victory. He dropped back into the pocket a found a receiver in the end zone and threw the ball. As he threw the ball a defensive back came from out of no where and intercepted the ball and began running toward his end zone for a touchdown. His only threat of being tackled came from the clumsy Georgia Tech quarterback. Eventually the quarterback saved the game for Georgia Tech and tackled the interceptor.

Following the game the coach from the opposing team asked Dodd how his clumsy quarterback was able to chased down his fastest defensive end. Dodd responded, "Your man was running for a touchdown, my man was running for his life."

He was motivated by fear. Others are motivated by affirmation.

Mark Twain dedicated his book *The Celebrated Jumping Frog* to John Smith, "who I have known at sundry places and whose many and manifold virtues did always command my esteem." Twain figured that their must be 1000's of John Smith's who would buy the book for the affirmation in its dedication. He was right. It made for a very profitable sale.

God shapes and molds our character through those who affirm us.

Fourth—God develops our character through those who oppose us. We should pay attention to those who oppose us and seek to learn from these negative circumstances.

David had opposition for the beginning.

Saul watched David. As David played the harp Saul hurled a javelin and tried to pin David to the wall. And David escaped twice. (I Samuel 18:9-11)

David learned from this opposition. His character was developed in the midst of Saul's opposition. In the end, David was a man who sought to do God's will and Saul was one who rebelled against God's will. David seemed to rise above his enemies. He wrote:

> The Lord is my light and my salvation; who shall I fear? The Lord is the strength of my life; of who shall I be afraid. (Psalm 27:1)

How about it? Are you taking seriously your responsibility to give guidance to others? Are you a true friend? Do you affirm others or tear them down? How do you treat those who oppose you? Do you lower yourself to their level or do you rise above? Let's re-think our commitment.

ALL PROPS REMOVED

I Samuel 19-21

And Saul spoke to Jonathan his son and to all his servants, that they should kill David.

In Grainger County, Tennessee there is a small Baptist church in the middle of a field. The building is made of concrete blocks that are painted white. On one side of the building someone has placed several two by fours to prop the wall. Evidently, they felt that without the props the wall would fall.

I often wondered how many props could be removed before the building would collapsed. 1, 2, 3? Maybe, just maybe, the building would not fall at all.

Props are good things to have in our lives. They give us support and security. Our career, family and friends are good examples of props that bring each of us satisfaction in life.

Props can also be bad. They can easily become crutches. Crutches hamper growth and become substitutes for God.

A promising young man was asked one time, "What do you want to get out of life?" He said, "I would like to finish college and get a good job."

"What then?" the young man was asked. "Oh, maybe settle down and get married and have a family," replied the young man.

"What then?" "See that my kids get through school and are on their own with their own families," was his response.

"What then?" "Oh, work a few more years and retire and enjoy traveling," said he.

"What then?" "Well, I suppose I'll die and be buried in the family cemetery," declared the man.

"What then?" There was no response from the young man.

The point is this—Our career, family and friends are good props but they are not good enough to be God. Where would your life be like if all of your props were removed? Have you allowed them to become crutches and allowed them to become substitutes for God?

In I Samuel 19 we see some props in David's life being removed. He had risen to great heights in the kingdom and everything seemed to be going great guns for him. Suddenly crisis struck. Never again would David be free from brokenness and pain. Through this brokenness and pain, David was forced to realize that the props in his life were not intended to be his God. He learned to depend on God and God alone.

We must learn to depend solely upon God. We can learn the hard way or the easy way. It was Isaiah who wrote:

> Do not fear for I am with you; Do not anxiously look about you,
> for I am your God. I will strengthen you, surely I will help you.
> Surely I will uphold you with my righteous right hand."

One by one David's props were removed until he had no one on which to lean. As we look at the props that are removed from his life, I invite you to examine your life and ask yourself the difficult question, "Am I trusting in the Lord, or am I trusting in a prop?" What would be your response if suddenly all the props were removed? Would your relationship with the Lord be sufficient to sustain your life?

Prop one: Position. David had moved up in the ranks. Just a few years had passed sense he was a mere shepherd boy. Now he had a prominent place in the military. He had led in battle as Saul's trusted officer.

> And there was war again; and David went out, and fought with
> the Philistines, and slew them with a great slaughter, and they fled
> from him. (I Samuel 19:8)

He had moved from slaying one Philistine to the slaughter of thousands. He was on his way to having a brilliant career as a military genius. Saul saw to it that David's career was thwarted.

Saul sought to pin David to the wall with a javelin, but he slipped
away out of Saul's presence, and he pinned the javelin into the wall.
And David fled . . . (I Samuel 19:10)

David no longer had the position he once enjoyed. He soon realized that
his position was a good prop but was not intended to be his God.

What would you do if it were not for your position? Is you entire life
built around your career? your position in our church or community?
What means more to you, your position or your relationship to God? Paul
says:

I count everything sheer loss, because all is far outweighed by the
gain of knowing Christ Jesus my Lord. (Philippians 3:8)

Prop two: Family. Saul was not content with David being gone, he wanted him
destroyed. He pursued David to his home. Michal, David's wife, protected
David by helping him to escape. She padded the blankets to make it look like
a man was lying in the bed and she told the messenger who came to capture
David that he was sick. Once again David fled. He no longer enjoyed the
presence of his family. He realized that his family was a good prop but was
not intended to be his God.

What would happen to you if your family was no longer yours to enjoy?
Would your relationship to God be sufficient to sustain your purpose for
living? Is your entire life built around your family or around God? Which
means more to you your family or your relationship to God? Jesus taught
that the love we have for our family should seem like hate when compared
to the love we have for God (Luke 14:26).

Prop three: Mentor. When David fled from Saul he went straight to Samuel,
his mentor. Samuel had anointed him as king and had always given him much
needed guidance. After David explained to Samuel the details of Saul's pursuit,
both he and Samuel fled to Naioth. Soon Saul discovered their hiding place
and David once again fled. David realized that his mentor was a good prop
but he was not intended to be his God.

What would happen to you if you no longer had the one around you
who gave you guidance? Would the guidance you receive from God be

able to sustain your life? Is your life built around human wisdom or God's wisdom?

Prop four: Friends. David fled from Naioth to Jonathan, his closest friend. In this scene we see that the bones of David's emotional security have begun to fissure. David asks his friend:

> What have I done? What is my iniquity? And what is my sin before
> your father, that he is seeking my life? (I Samuel 20:1)

Jonathan assures David that he will not die. At this point David is not comforted. Saul's fiery eyes and the whir of the hurled spear is still fresh on his mind. Because of the danger, Jonathan and David decided to part. Perhaps this was David's most painful loss. David would never see Jonathan again. He fled to Gath. No position, no family, no mentor, nor friends, all of these were good props but they were not intended to be his God.

What would happen if your friends were suddenly removed from your life? Would your current friendship with God be sufficient to sustain your life? Have you built your life around your friends instead of God?

Prop Five: Self-Respect. It seems that David could not go anywhere without being recognized. He was immediately recognized in Goliath's hometown. David's desperation swelled as he was once again seized by fear. Take a look at the demeaning act he put on:

> And he changed his behavior before them, and feigned himself mad
> in their hands, and made marks on the doors of the gate, and let
> his spittle run down his beard. (I Samuel 21:13)

David had lost all he once had no career, no family, no friend, no mentor, not even self respect. There he was in a cave . . . all alone . . . just him . . . and God. No props, just God.

The great preacher Jonathan Edwards was a man who was totally sold out to God. One who did not depend on props to be his God. He wrote:

> I claim no right to myself—no right to this understanding, this
> will, these affections that are in me: neither do I have any right to
> this body or its members—no right to this tongue, to these hands,
> feet, ears, eyes.

I have given myself clear away and not retained anything of my own. I have been to God this morning and told Him I have given myself wholly to Him. I have given every power, so that for the future I claim no right to myself in any respect. I have expressly promised Him, for by His grace I will not fail. I take Him as my whole portion and felicity, looking upon nothing else as any part of my happiness. His law is the constant rule of my obedience.

I will fight with all my against the world, the flesh, and the devil to the end of my life. I will adhere to the faith of the Gospel, however hazardous and difficult the profession and practice of it may be.

If I murmur in the least at afflictions; if I am in any way uncharitable; if I revenge my own case; if I do anything purely to please myself, or omit anything because it is a great denial; if I trust myself; if I take any praise for any good which Christ does by me; or if I am any way proud, I shall act as my own and not God's. I purpose to be absolutely His.

There is an important lesson here for us to learn. We know with our hearts that God and God alone is worthy of our life but day in and day out we place our hope on temporary things. Careers will one day fail us. Family one day will be gone. Mentors will not be around forever. Friends will fail. Our own self-respect will not suffice. Where will you turn? Can you honestly say that you are trusting in the Lord with all your heart or are you only being temporally propped by your understanding?

LIFE'S MOST SUBTLE TEMPTATION

I Samuel 24

When Saul returned from following the Philistines, he was told, 'David is in the wilderness of En-gedi.' Then Saul took three thousand chosen men out of all Israel, and went to look for David and his men in the direction of the Rocks of the Wild Goats. He came to the sheepfolds beside the road, where there was a cave; and Saul went in to relieve himself.

Now David and his men were sitting in the innermost parts of the cave. The men of David said to him, 'Here is the day of which the Lord said to you, "I will give your enemy into your hand, and you shall do to him as it seems good to you."' Then David went and stealthily cut off a corner of Saul's cloak. Afterwards David was stricken to the heart because he had cut off a corner of Saul's cloak. He said to his men, 'The Lord forbid that I should do this thing to my lord, the Lord's anointed, to raise my hand against him; for he is the Lord's anointed.' So David scolded his men severely and did not permit them to attack Saul. Then Saul got up and left the cave, and went on his way.

In *Othello*, Shakespeare vividly portrays a universal temptation which tries to entrap us in its thistly branches.

Iago, ensign of the Venetian army, hates his general, Othello. When Othello promotes young and handsome Cassio over him, Iago plants a thicket of lies to ensnare Othello in the thorns of revenge.

Iago begins his plot by planting a seed of distrust in Othello's mind concerning his bride's faithfulness, framing Cassio as her lover. This tiny seed of jealousy sprouts into a tangled, tragic nightmare. Iago's plan is consummated when he murders a man and wounds Cassio and Othello suffocates his innocent bride, Desdemona and takes his own life.

Lies, murder, suicide occurred because of Iago's frustrated ambition, his hunger for power, and his slighted pride.

Like, Iago, David must have felt that his superior, Saul, had wronged him. Out of jealousy and anger, Saul had reduced David's position from right-hand man to refugee.

In I Samuel 24 we find David with an opportunity to give Saul a bitter taste of revenge or a sweet savor of reconciliation. David had a choice to make.

Would he kill Saul and receive the plaudits of his men or would he spare Saul and receive plaudits of his God? Would he seek revenge or reconciliation?

Revenge or reconciliation? It seems that humanity is often torn between the two. Revenge says, "I have my rights and I'll make him/her pay!" Reconciliation says, "What can I do to help bring healing." Both revenge and reconciliation seek the same end. Revenge says, "Destroy your enemies by getting even with them." Reconciliation says, "Destroy your enemies by making them your friend."

Sometimes we are ambivalent about revenge, but God is not. Paul wrote:

> Never pay back evil for evil to anyone. Respect what is right in the sight of all men. If possible, so far as it depends on you, be at peace with all men. Never take you own revenge, beloved, but leave room for the wrath of God, for it is written, "Vengeance of mine, I will repay," says the Lord. (Romans 12:17-19)

If there is any vengeance, God commands us to leave it in His hands. As far as we are concerned we are to seek peace and reconciliation.

How do you deal with the Saul's in your life? Are you vengeful or forgiving? Do you seek to hurt or to heal?

When we last looked a David's life we found him at one of the lowest points in his life. He was down and out, questioning why these things were happening to him. David surrounded himself with a band of men and he became their captain. David and his men saved the town of Keilah from the Philistines, fled from Saul and his army, and had been saved by the bell when a Philistine raid took Sauls attention off of David.

Now we find David and his company safely camouflaged in the cool cave of Engedi, but tenacious Saul gets wind of David's whereabouts. Saul took three thousand crack troops to capture David. It's clear that Saul meant business.

While in pursuit of David, Saul stepped into a cave. Little did he know that David and his men were hiding in the darkness. For the first time since Saul began to purse David, Saul was vulnerable.

The men who were with David began to advise David to take revenge. Their human nature went into overdrive. They felt the Lord had delivered Saul into their hands for that purpose. Isn't it interesting how the men cloaked their revenge in spirituality?

Often God gets the blame for things of which he has nothing to do. There was agreement that God had placed Saul into their mercy but their was disagreement about what God had intended for them to do. David soldiers excused their desire to get even with Saul by saying it was God's timing, His will.

What about you? Are you harboring an attitude or a desire to get even because you feel it is God's way for you? Are you harboring resentment towards someone because you feel God is on your side?

David heard the voices of his men that day. The clamor of their opinions didn't persuade him to do what was wrong. There was another voice that was speaking to David that day. It was the voice of God. While the voices of the men were shouting, "Now is your chance, seek retaliation!" God said, "Now is your chance, seek reconciliation!"

There was a better way for David. It was the way of peace, forgiveness and integrity. It was a way after God's heart.

David could kill Saul and instantly become the monarch of Israel. He knew that he needed to trust in God's timing and not in his own. However, he could not pass up this chance to get Saul. He had to come close enough to Saul to get a least a taste of the sweetness of revenge.

Because David was so conscious of his relationship to God, certain things took place when he tuned to God's heart and listened to Him. These same things will happen for us when we heed to God's voice.

When we are in tune with God's heart we will become sensitive to our own heart. We will become aware of our shortcomings as we listen to God.

David had barely slid the knife back into its sheath when God pricked his conscience. David's heart smote him and he said:

> The Lord forbid that I should do this thing to my master, the Lord's
> anointed, to stretch forth my hand against him. (I Samuel 24:6)

David was sensitive to the resounding chords of his heart. He became aware through the pricking of his conscience that he had done something that was not in accordance with God's will.

When we are in tune with God's heart we will seek to forgive those who have done us wrong. We will discover a better way, a higher road.

> David arose and came out of the cave and cried unto Saul, saying, My lord, my king. And when Saul looked behind him, David stooped with his face to the earth, and bowed himself. (I Samuel 24:8)

David went beyond the call of duty. He did everything he knew to make peace with Saul, his adversary.

Many times when you and I are wronged we write the transgression in stone or bronze never intending to forget the hurt. When you and I wrong others we expect the other person to write the offense in sand or in the air. Yet, when we wrong God he stands eagerly awaiting to forgive us.

Peter asked Jesus one day how many times we are to forgive others. Jesus' response was that we are to forgive as many times as is necessary for healing. And you remember the model prayer where Jesus taught us to pray, "Forgive us our trespasses as we forgive those who trespass against us."

Do you request forgiveness from God while holding a grudge against someone else? Are you ready to seek reconciliation or revenge?

Leonardo Da Vinci had a violent quarrel with one of his dearest friends before he began painting the Last Supper. He determined that he would paint the likeness of his friend as the face of Judas and he did. When he began to paint the face of Christ his creative juices stopped. He could not paint any longer. He realized his guilt over the painting of his friend's face for Judas and corrected his sin. Then he received his creativity and completed the face of Jesus.

The point is this—You cannot at one and the same time be painting the features of Christ in your own life and be painting the face of others with enmity and strife. "Lord, forgive us our trespasses AS we those who trespass against us."

There was a time when God had been trespassed against. We were the ones guilty of sin. God met us and had a choice to make. He could either ball his fist to retaliate or he could open his arms to forgive. Fortunately for us He choose the latter. He sent his only son Jesus for a payment for our lives.

When we are in tune with God's heart we will seek to please him. The writer of Proverbs 16:7 has something to say to us. "When a man's ways please God, he maketh his enemies to be at peace with him." It makes God happy when we seek reconciliation with those who offend us. What about it? Is your life pleasing God?

CLOUDY DAYS . . . . DARK NIGHTS

I Samuel 27

David said in his heart, 'I shall now perish one day by the hand of Saul; there is nothing better for me than to escape to the land of the Philistines; then Saul will despair of seeking me any longer within the borders of Israel, and I shall escape out of his hand.' So David set out and went over, he and the six hundred men who were with him, to King Achish son of Maoch of Gath. David stayed with Achish at Gath, he and his troops, every man with his household, and David with his two wives, Ahinoam of Jezreel, and Abigail of Carmel, Nabal's widow. When Saul was told that David had fled to Gath, he no longer sought for him.

The Pilgrim's Progress, a literary classic, was written by John Bunyan while he was in prison for preaching the gospel without a license. It is an allegory of the Christian life. In his book he teaches his readers how to handle cloudy days and dark nights through a pilgrim named Christian.

While traveling to the Celestial City, Christian falls into a bog, a deep miry muddy hole called the Slough of Despond. His loyal friend and traveling companion, Pliable, finds his way out and goes home and leaves Christian to struggle alone in the slough. As he struggles, he cries for help and finally the Holy Spirit comes and pulls his out of the Slough of Despond. The Holy Spirit sets Christian on his feet and wipes the slime of despondency off his brow.

Each of us spend time in that muddy hole. We have times when we see no hope and we are tempted to give up. We have times when we can't see past the clouds in the sky. It seems that the more we do to try to come out of the muddy hole the further down we sink. Even though there is nothing morally, ethically or spiritually wrong with feeling the deep pangs of despair, it's when we try to find our own way out that we have problems. It's like a corkscrew, the harder we try with our own resources the further down we go.

David certainly had times like these. In I Samuel 27 we find an episode of disobedience in his life. He was down, again. This time he tried to find his own way out and ran for cover in the enemy camp. What did he do that we need to avoid? How can we prevent falling deeper and deeper in the muck and mire of the cloudy days and dark nights? We do not have to dash toward disobedience.

David's dash toward disobedience started with distorting thinking. The Bible says out of the heart comes the issues of life. David's mind was distorted. He only saw his perspective.

David was own a roller coaster high. Twice he could have killed Saul and twice he passed the chance by. He wanted to kill Nabal but was talked out of it by Abigail. He was feeling righteous and victorious. He was vulnerable to self's seductive voice.

> There is nothing wrong with talking to yourself. Just make sure that what you respond to are the right things. David responded to the wrong things that he was saying to himself. All he could see was a wall. Not once in this chapter does he seek God's perspective and advice.

His reasoning was clouded with pessimism. He had his paintbrush out and he was painting his horizon black. All the people who had had influence in his life had said positive things about his future. Samuel anointed David to be King of Israel one day. Jonathan who was supposed to be king said to David, "You are next in line to the throne." Abigail, his new bride, knew that David would be king. Even his enemy, Saul had once said, "I know that I am looking at my replacement." David, pious hero on the outside, was a pouting doubter on the inside. He felt that one day he would die at the hands of Saul.

His logic was strictly rational. He could think of nothing better to do than to go with the enemy. He says:

> There is nothing better for me to do than that I should speedily escape in the land of the Philistines, and Saul shall despair of me, to seek me any more in any border of Israel. So shall I escape out of his hand. (I Samuel 27:1c)

This story is a perfect example of destruction beginning with what we think. Every sin that is committed begins with our thinking. No murder has been committed without first being thought about. No harsh word has ever been spoken that was not first thought.

David's dash toward disobedience had some serious consequences.

He brought others with him. Maybe he didn't invite them but they came. All 600 of them. He had trained them and they looked up to him and followed him.

Who are you bringing with you? No one lives unto themselves, nor dies to themselves, nor sins to themselves. Like David, we have a circle of people who follow our lead. We will be accountable for how we took that responsibility.

He had a false sense of security. Disobedience should bring remorse, but more often it brings exhilaration. That's how David felt. Saul called off the search for David and when he did I am sure David let out one huge sigh of relief. True, sin has its pleasures, but they are passing. David felt safe in Philistia but destruction was around the corner. When we are disobedient we will think everything is all right when in fact it isn't.

He went through a period of compromise. The longer he splashed around in the bog the less he wanted to get out. He spent sixteen months in Philistia and in that period of time no psalms were ever written.

Mullah, an ancient Persian humorist, and his son were walking down a road with their donkey grazing in front of them. As they walked they would pass various groups of people. One man said, "Look how foolish they are, walking instead of riding their donkey!" Hearing the remark of the man, Mullah and his son got on the donkey and rode it to the next village. As they entered the village a woman shouted, "They ought to be ashamed making that Donkey carry two riders!" Hearing these words Mullah dismounted and let his son ride the donkey. As they continued to travel another woman said, "Poor old man. That boy should be ashamed making his father walk while he rides the donkey. So mullah gets on the donkey and his son walks. They continued on their journey and another man shouted, "Look at that old man riding while he make his son walk!" Mullah rubbed his beard and said, "You can't please any of the people all the time." Then he picked up the donkey carried it the rest of the journey. Compromise is a common result of disobedience.

Duplicity, vagueness and secrecy became a part of David's life. David couldn't see the storm brewing. The clouds became darker and darker. Soon David was knee deep in muddy mistakes. He was Israelite at heart but had to act like a Philistine.

> David saved neither man nor woman alive, to bring tidings to Gath, saying, Lest they should tell on us, saying, So did David, and so will be his manner all the while he dwelleth in the country of the Philistines. (I Samuel 27:11)

David's dash toward disobedience brought destruction. He finally had his secrets found out. He could no longer compromise and be an Israelite.

David was displaced. He was neither Israelite or Philistine. He had fooled Achish but not his commanders.

> And the commanders of Philistia were angry with him; and the princes of the Philistines said unto Achish, Make this fellow return, that he may go to his place which thou hast appointed him, and let him not go down into battle, lest he become our adversary. (I Samuel 29:4)

He was distrusted and in distress. David was sinking deeper and deeper. David was at the bottom. What a tangled web we weave when we practice to deceive.

> David was greatly distressed; for the people spoke of stoning him. Because the soul of the people was grieved. (I Samuel 29:6)

Fortunately David's destruction was not final. He finally pulled back the cloud and saw God standing, waiting patiently. The text says that David encouraged himself in the Lord.

How about it? Have your tired feet slipped and slid into despair because you have tried to manage your life without God? Have you lived the last few days, weeks or months as if their were no God? David would say "You don't have to have cloudy days and dark nights any longer. Pull back the clouds and look to God for help!"

A MAN WHO FLED FROM GOD'S HEART

I Samuel 31

Now the Philistines fought against Israel; and the men of Israel fled before the Philistines, and many fell on Mount Gilboa. The Philistines overtook Saul and his sons; and the Philistines killed Jonathan and Abinadab and Malchishua, the sons of Saul. The battle pressed hard upon Saul; the archers found him, and he was badly wounded by them. Then Saul said to his armour-bearer, 'Draw your sword and thrust me through with it, so that these uncircumcised may not come and thrust me through, and make sport of me.' But his armour-bearer was unwilling; for he was terrified. So Saul took his own sword and fell upon it. When his armour-bearer saw that Saul was dead, he also fell upon his sword and died with him. So Saul and his three sons and his armour-bearer and all his men died together on the same day. When the men of Israel who were on the other side of the valley and those beyond the Jordan saw that the men of Israel had fled and that Saul and his sons were dead, they forsook their towns and fled; and the Philistines came and occupied them.

If you had the opportunity to write the epitaph for your grave marker, what would it be? What words would you use to describe your life?

Sometimes epitaphs are humorous. Allow me to mention a few that I have read.

Here lies my wife in earthy mold who when she lived did naught but scold: Good friends go softly in your walking lest she would wake and rise up talking.

On the four husbands of Ivy Saunders one finds:

Here lie my husbands 1-2-3 as still as men could ever be: As for the fourth: Praise be to God he still abides above the sod: Abel, Seth: and Leidy were the first 3 names and to make things tidy I'll add his—James.

or:

Beneath this stone a lump of clay lies Uncle Peter Daniels: Too early in the month of May he took off his winter flannels.

and one more that was on a hypochondriac's tombstone:

I told you I was sick.

How would you summarize your life? Would you characterize it as meaningful or meaningless? Do you feel as if your life is abundant?

In I Samuel 31 we find the record of the death of Saul. If we were to affix an epitaph for a tombstone for his grave it could read: "Behold, I have played a fool," or "A Man Who Fled from God's Heart."

Few men have had beginnings as bright as Saul's. Physically, emotionally, spiritually, professionally, he had it all. Yet from that high and noble beginning, Saul sank to an infamous ending. Saul lived a meaningless life. The pathetic way in which he died mirrors a kind of life that was empty and void.

In Shakespeare's *Macbeth*, we hear Macbeth sobbing these words about his meaningless life:

Life's but a walking shadow, a poor player that struts and frets his hour upon the stage and then is heard no more: it is a tale told by an idiot, full of sound and fury, signifying nothing.

It is a sad commentary on our world that many people are not living but existing. It is not a rich-poor issue. It is not a black-white issue. It is not associated with one's environment. It can exist in the slums of Harlem as well as in the suites on Park Avenue. Some people live life as if God created them a little above the animals rather than a little below himself. It is even sadder to note that people who live a meaningless do not have to. Jesus came to give us abundant life. Yet, we seem to settle for mediocrity.

What are some characteristics of a mediocre life? How can we live life in a meaningful way? How can we avoid meaninglessness? Let's talk a look at some of the characteristics of Saul's meaningless life and compare them with our own life.

First—When we are more concerned with what man thinks of us rather than what God thinks of us, life is meaningless.

Even when facing death, Saul's main concern was to preserve his image in the eyes of the enemy. Listen to his last words:

> Draw thy sword, and thrust me through, lest these uncircumcised
> come and thrust me through and abuse me. (I Samuel 31:4)

Saul offered no prayer of repentance, no plea for help. His eyes were fixed on a horizontal plane of carnality and on that plane he died.

If you were to die today, which image would you try to preserve—an image of someone tough and impregnable in the eyes of the world or of one repentant and forgiven in the eyes of God?

Second—When we do not recognize God in our life, life is meaningless. When we flee from God's heart our life can be nothing but empty and void of meaning.

It matters not how you slice the pieces of Saul's life, he was a failure. His failure was not due to the lack of ability nor Israel's weakness but because of his refusal to be obedient to the will of God.

David was characterized as own who was after God's heart. Anything David felt that God wanted him to be or to do, David tried to accomplish. Granted, he messed up royally sometimes. Nevertheless, David's heartfelt desire was to please God.

Saul was completely the opposite. If God told him to do something, Saul would either ignore it or do the opposite. If God had told Saul to paint a fence black he would have painted it white. If God had told Saul to buy a truck to haul the Israelites around he would have bought a car and made the Israelites walk! If God said "Go Up!", Saul would have gone down. If you are not in the center of God's will for your life you will not find the meaningfulness that God intends for you to have.

Third—When we see life as trouble to be avoided rather than challenges to be met, life is meaningless. We sometimes focus on what we cannot do and forget all that we can do.

One of the tragedies of the 1988 Olympics was the story of Ben Johnson of Canada. As you remember, he was billed as the fastest man in the world, He was said to be faster than Carl Lewis of the United States.

You will also remember that Johnson was disqualified when it was discovered that he used antibolic steroids to enhance his bodily strength. He was so concerned with the possibility of failure or what he felt he could not do, he took matters into his own hands. The tragedy is that he might have won with the steroids. His efforts were meaningless because he faced the race as trouble to be avoided rather than a challenge to be met.

Fourth—When we define living in terms of our own existence, life is meaningless. All Saul could see was the cloud of disaster. He could not see God there behind it. He could not see that the same things that were at David's disposal was at his too.

In his book, *The Age of Anxiety*, William Auden writes about the man who sees life only from the perspective of his own existence. He writes:

> He is tired out; His last illusions have lost patience with the human enterprise. The end comes: he joins the majority, the jaw-dropped, mildewed mob and is modest at last.

When life is meaningless we will reach a point of utter and cynical despair.

Fifth—When life is meaningless we can find meaning in our Savior.

Dr. Frank Hawkins, pastor of the First Baptist Church of Kingsport, Tennessee, tells the story of taking his son to a carnival. He recalls that while he was there his son would come back again and again for more tickets to ride the rides.

Later in the afternoon, other little boys would come to get tickets. Frank would explain to them that the tickets were his son's and not theirs to enjoy.

The boys responded by saying, "We know, he said to come to you for some tickets."

Jesus says, "Come to my Father, he'll give you what you need!"

In the great work of Carl Sandburg, *Abraham Lincoln: The War Years*, he discusses the darkest years of Lincoln's life. He traces the events that led to one of the saddest points in American history, Lincoln's assassination.

He draws the title of one of the chapters from an old woodman's proverb: A tree is best measured when it's down. His point is this—It took the felling of this great man for us to appreciate his solid-oak character.

From the tips of the roots to the very top branch, how would you measure your life. Is it like David's, as one who is after God's heart or is it like Saul's, empty and void of meaning? If you find your life is meaningless there really is hope. Come and see for yourself.

DAVID AND THE ARK

II Samuel 6

David again gathered all the chosen men of Israel, thirty thousand. David and all the people with him set out and went from Baale-judah, to bring up from there the ark of God, which is called by the name of the Lord of hosts who is enthroned on the cherubim. They carried the ark of God on a new cart, and brought it out of the house of Abinadab, which was on the hill. Uzzah and Ahio the sons of Abinadab, were driving the new cart with the ark of God;and brought it out of the house of Abinadab, which was on the hill with the ark of God and Ahio went in front of the ark. David and all the house of Israel were dancing before the Lord with all their might, with songs and lyres and harps and tambourines and castanets and cymbals.

"Then Jesus took his disciples up the mountain and gathering around him, he taught them saying:

Blessed are the poor in spirit, for theirs is the kingdom of heaven.
Blessed are the meek.
Blessed are they that mourn.
Blessed are the merciful.
Blessed are they who thirst for justice.
Blessed are you when persecuted.
Blessed are you when you suffer.
Be glad and rejoice for your reward is great in heaven.
Then Simon Peter said . . . .

Do we have to write this down?
And Andrew said . . . .
Are we supposed to know this?
And James said . . .
Will we have a test on this?
And Philip said . . . .
I don't have any paper.
And Bartholomew said . . . .
Do we have to turn this in?
And John said . . .
The other disciples didn't have to learn this.
And Matthew said . . . .
Can I go to the boy's room?
And Judas said . . . .
What does this have to do with the real world?
Then one of the Pharisees who was present asked to see Jesus's lesson plan and inquired of Jesus . . .

Where is your anticipatory set and your objectives in this cognitive domain?

And Jesus wept.

Details! They are a part of life but just like the disciples we do not know how to deal with them at times. Which ones can we ignore and which ones should we remember?

Israel had become spiritually malnourished under Saul's reign. The tabernacle had deteriorated, its furnishings had been scattered, the worship had become virtually meaningless. Since God's presence was associated with the tabernacle furnishings, the people of Israel no longer felt his nearness. As Israel's new king, David wanted to re-establish the center of worship. He wanted to renew his people's fear of God and fatten their spiritual fervor.

David once again displays that his life pulsed to the heartbeat of God. He was committed to obeying the Lord God of hosts. He was Man after God's own heart.

The theme of this chapter is a theme that we have heard before. But it is a theme that we need to hear over and over. We need to apply to our Life what King David knew about God's will. How can we know if we are a person after God's own heart? How can we know if we take God's will seriously? Is your heart linked to God's heart or does your heart follow a different agenda than that of God? For you see, the better you know where you stand with the Lord, the freer you can be.

II Samuel 6 tells us a interesting story about David and the Ark of the Covenant. It is not only a story about David, Uzzah and Michal. It is a story about us. This morning I invite you look in a spiritual mirror and see if the characteristics of your life matche that of the characteristics of one whose life is pulsing to the heartbeat of God.

First—If our life pulses to the heartbeat of God, we will know where to meet Him.

King David knew that the existence of his new kingdom depended on strong center of worship. He knew that meant gathering the articles of the tabernacle, particularly the Ark of the Covenant. The Ark of the Covenant was the very place that God met His people.

> And David arose, and went with all the people who were with him from Ba'ale-judah, to bring up from there the ark of God, whose name is called by the name of the Lord of hosts who dwelleth between the cherubims. (II Samuel 6:2)

The ark was a chest of acacia wood, gold plated inside and out. It was rimmed with a border of Gold. It was over three feet long, two feet wide and two feet high. Its pure gold lid, the mercy seat, held two cherubs of hammered gold with wings outstretched over the cover. It contained only three objects: A golden jar containing manna, Aaron's rod, and the Ten Commandments. It was the most important part of the tabernacle.

Even before the cross worship was highly symbolic. When the Israelites looked at the ark, they saw more than a box made from acacia wood and gold. They saw holiness . . . the very glory of God.

Although there is no longer a tabernacle, an ark of the covenant, or a holy of holies, God's presence is still found in a valuable vessel. This vessel is our heart.

We are creatures that have an incredible thirst and hunger for God. Augustine of Hippo once prayed:

> O God, thou hast made us for thyself and our Souls are restless, searching, 'til they find their rest in thee.

King David knew where to meet God. He knew that his wholeness depended on knowing where to find God. As you look in the mirror do you see a person that knows where to meet God? Is your life pulsing at the heartbeat of God? Paul wrote:

> And what agreement hath the temple of God with idols? for you are the temple of the living God; as God hath said, I will dwell in them, and walk in them; and I will be their God, and they shall be my people. (II Corinthians 6:16)

Second—If your life pulses to the heartbeat of God, we will respect His holiness and will follow His precepts. In his zeal to bring the ark to Jerusalem, David overlooked God's instructions on how to transport it, bringing it instead on the wheels of haste and convenience.

And they placed the ark of God on a new cart that they might bring it from the house of Abinadab which was on a hill; and Uzzah and Ahio were leading the cart . . . But when they came to the threshing floor of Nacon, Uzzah reached out toward the ark of God and took hold of it for the oxen nearly upset it. And the anger of the Lord burned against Uzzah, and God struck him down for his irreverence; and he died their by the ark of God. (I Samuel 6:3,6-7)

Instead of being carried on the shoulders of Levites, the ark was carried on a cart. and instead of revering the ark, Uzzah touched it, desecrating its holiness. Clearly, David had overlooked the details of God's plan, details so important to God that He took Uzzah's life.

There is no doubt that Uzzah had the best of intentions. But he did the right thing in the wrong way. The means did not justify the end. John Newton said, "If you think you see the ark of God falling you can be quite sure that it is due to a swimming in your own head!"

God has given us general principles as well as specific precepts to follow. We ourselves will be stricken for our sincere but half hearted attempts to do His will. Some say it doesn't matter what a person believes as long as he or she is sincere. I am sure that would be very comforting to Uzzah. One cannot go down a wrong road in life with good intentions and expect to end up where God wants. Our sincerity only matters when we follow God's precepts, the specific plan of God for our life.

How about it? Are you banking on God to accept you because of your intentions? I hope you are depending on the grace of God through Jesus Christ as your way to God? Is your life pulsing to the heartbeat of God?

Third—If your life is pulsing to the heartbeat of God, you will fear Him. Do you live life with the awareness of God's presence?

As Uzzah's body lay alongside the ark, David's anger burned against God, until an awareness of God's presence gripped his raging heart and turned him back.

> And David became angry because of the Lord's outburst against Uzzah. So David was afraid of the Lord that day; and said, "How can the ark of the Lord come to me?" (II Samuel 6:3-9)

David was not perfect. But he was sensitive to sin. He admitted his wrong and began to take God seriously. He humbly refused to move the ark to Jerusalem and took it to the house Obed-edom instead.

During the three months the ark was with Obed-edom. David watched the blessing it brought to his house, which made David eager to bring it to Jerusalem.

What happened to make David change his mind? The answer: he did his homework. He discovered the proper way to carry the ark. He said to the Levites:

> Because you did not carry it at the first, the Lord, our God made an outburst on us, for we did not seek Him according to the ordinance. (I Chronicles 15:13)

King David not only admitted his wrong, the next time around he made it right. He instructed the Levites that they were to carry the ark on their shoulders, with the poles that the Lord had instructed them to have.

When it comes to obeying God, it's the details, the rings and the poles, that snag us. Either we don't want to go to the trouble of getting the poles, or we don't want to carry them upon our shoulders. So we grab a cart, rewrite the rules and do our own way.

Are there some rings and poles that you have been ignoring? What are the details of God's will you have been ignoring? Your study life? Your prayer life? Your church life? Being a child of God means more than just being aware of the details. It means doing those things God wants you to do, caring for the things God wants you to care for, grieving over what grieve him, being willing to do His will, His way.

As you look at your life do you see someone who fears God? Are continuously aware of his presence? Is your life pulsing to the heartbeat of God?

Fourth—If your life is pulsing to the heartbeat of God, you will have a deep wisdom of what it means to be free.

Some might think that following every detail of God's will would make you unbending and stern. But this wasn't the case with David. When he followed the detail of God we find that David was anything but rigid.

> And David was dancing before the Lord with all his might, and David was wearing a linen ephod. So David and all of the house of Israel were bringing up the ark of the Lord with shouting and the sound of the trumpet. (II Samuel 6:14-15)

For David, it was more than a religious rite. It was the release from his remorse; the restoration of his joy in the Lord after profound repentance; the liberation of his whole person from fear of having offended the Almighty. He acknowledged that God once deigned to come and dwell among his people.

During the celebration, David composed one of his most magnificent psalms. Few others match this one for the honor, praise and majesty poured out upon God. (I Chronicles 16:7ff).

Do you have a deep wisdom of what it means to be free? If not, place your burden in the hands of God and begin to experience what it means to be free instead of in bondage.

How does your life compare to that of what God would have? Every direction has a destination. In 5, 10, 15 years you will have made it. The question is where? Will your life be one that pulses to the heartbeat of God?

WHEN GOD SAYS NO

II Samuel 7

Now when the king was settled in his house, and the Lord had given him rest from all his enemies around him, the king said to the prophet Nathan, 'See now, I am living in a house of cedar, but the ark of God stays in a tent.' Nathan said to the king, 'Go, do all that you have in mind; for the Lord is with you.'

How many times a day do you see a sign that says, "No"? A sign that reads 35 mph says no. No, you cannot drive faster than 35 mph. We have "No Parking" signs, "No walking" signs and the list goes on.

Ready on the tongue of every parent is the bread and butter word, no, the mere word that stops children in their tracks. No, don't touch that hot stove. No, don't jump on the bed. No, don't put those marbles in your mouth.

Today we will look at a time when God stamped the box of David's dream with a bold black no. And we'll see how David handled it. We will see whether David ran from God in disillusionment or to Him in contentment and trust.

So far, David's life has been like a great symphony that flows from one passionate movement to another. But in II Samuel 7, it pauses to play a tranquil strain. Finally, the courageous warrior is allowed to rest. For the first time in the new king dom there was peace. The Philistines had finally been driven out of Israel's territory.

David nestled back in his beautiful cedar house and began to entertain a dream. He dreams of building a temple for the ark of God. David confides in his counselor, the prophet Nathan.

> See now, I dwell in a house of cedar, but the ark of God dwells within tent curtains. (II Samuel 7:2)

There was nothing wrong with David's dream. Building a temple for the ark of the covenant was David's way of doing something for the Lord God of hosts who had done so much for him. The God who had led him from the role of a shepherd to that of a king. God in his wisdom said, "No."

David must have been surprised by God's refusal of his dream. We can learn from David's reaction. How do you deal with the word, "No"? Do you give up on everything that God offers because he shuts a door? Let's glean from these verses some truths that will help us when God says no.

The first truth is this—When God says no, we may hear yes from others. People that we trust may give us the wrong advice.

David tells his closest advisor, Nathan, of his dream. David's eyes must have been beaming with anticipation. Nathan speaks too soon. He puts words in God's mouth.

Nathan says:

> Go, do all that is within your mind, for the Lord is with you. (II Samuel 7:3)

It is often during the quiet interludes of our life, the times when we slow down and reflect on our past, that we find new direction, new hope, new dreams for the future. Yet, just because we have pulled back from the rat race doesn't mean that every dream is from God, not even admirable dreams, even though God's people may affirm their value.

David may have gotten the go-ahead from Nathan, but the final word came from God. Only He knows His plan for our lives.

Friends, family, and the church, are all good ways to help us to determine what God's will is for us. In fact, these are some of the primary ways of discerning His will. But in the final analysis we are responsible for what we have heard and accountable to God for what we have done. The judgment of the church or friends or family will not matter in the end. It is God's thinking to which we will be held accountable.

Sometimes God says yes when our closest advisors say no. Sometimes we have to distinguish between the wisdom of man and the Wisdom of God. When it all comes down to a decision, YOU are the one responsible and accountable for your decisions and actions.

The second truth is this—When God says no, it means redirection, not rejection. It means that God has a greater purpose for you to achieve.

God responded to David's dream with a gracious refusal and a prophetic word. In the night, God spoke to Nathan the prophet saying:

> Go and tell David my servant, Thus saith the Lord, You shall not build a house for me to dwell in." (I Chronicles 17:3-4)

God's refusal was not a rejection, but a redirection. God had a different dream. Instead of David building God a house, God promised David that he was going to build him a house, a dynasty that would last for years.

God didn't gift David as a builder, but as a soldier and king. There was nothing wrong with David's dream. His motives were pure; his intentions, pleasing to God. But he wasn't the right man to carry out the plan. God wanted a man of peace to build his temple. He saw that the greatest thing David could do was to lead the people to resolve their problems as a new nation.

God can be trusted to lead our lives. The poet said it well.

> Tis far, far better to let Him choose the way that we should take;
> If only we leave our lives to him He will guide without mistake.
> We, in our blindness, would never choose a pathway dark and rough.
> And so we should never find in Him, "The God Who is Enough."

Oliver Cromwell's secretary was dispatched to the continent on some important business. He stayed one night at the seaport town, and tossed and turned in his bed, unable to sleep.

According to an old custom, a servant slept in his room, and on this occasion slept soundly enough. The secretary at length awakened the man who asked how it was that his master could not rest.

I am so afraid something will fo wrong with the trip," was the reply.

"master," said the valet, "may I ask a question or two?"

"Did God rule the world before we were born?"

"Most assuredly he did."

"And will He rule it after we are dead?"

"Certainly He will."

"Then, master, why not let Him rule the present, too?

The secretary's faith was stirred, peace was the result, and in a few minutes both he and his servant were in sound sleep.

Has God ever said no to your dreams? A dream of going to the mission field . . . of marrying someone with whom you felt you were destined to be . . . of landing that promotion which was rightfully yours? These kind of mysterious no's are difficult to handle. If you believe that God really loves you, really wants what is best for you, if you trust him for what's best in your life, He will show you the better plan he has for you.

> I know the thoughts that I have toward you, saith the Lord, thoughts of peace, and not evil, to give you an expected end. (Jeremiah 29:11)

The third truth is this—When God says no, we must realize that he knows us fully.

Like a humbled child, David expresses his trust in God's knowledge of his heart. He says to God:

> Who am I, O Lord God? And what is my house, that thou hast brought me this far? And what can David say more unto thee? For thou, Lord, knowest thy servant. (II Samuel 7:18-20)

It was a comfort to David that God knew him fully. God knew his capabilities and achievements. He knew his motives and attitudes. We should respond to situations like David responded. We must acknowledge His wisdom for our life even when He does something for us the way we least expect it to be done.

There was once a hitchhiker traveling around Chicago when it was only 20 degrees. As he was standing on the side of the road with the snowy air blowing on his cold exposed thumb, he began to wonder if he would ever get a ride.

In his despair, he saw an approaching car indicating that it was going to stop for him. As the car passed, the passenger's window was rolled down and a pair of gloves was hurled out to him.

As he put on the gloves, he waved thank you and continued hitchhiking.

Sometimes God meets our need in unusual ways and we must respond like the hitchhiker by saying, "Lord, that's not what I was expecting but thank you."

The fourth truth is this—When God says no, we must recommit to his will for our life. David's response to God's no was godly, gracious and full of trust.

And now, O Lord God, the word that thou hast spoken concerning thy servant, and concerning his house, establish it forever, and do as thou hast said. (II Samuel 7:25)

George W. Truett was entertained on one occasion in the home of a wealthy oil man in Texas. After the dinner the man took him up to the roof of the house and indicated a huge field of oil derricks and said, "Dr. Truett, that's all mine, I came to this country twenty five years ago, penniless, and now I own everything as far as you can see in that direction. Then he turned to the opposite direction and indicated waving fields of grain and said again, It's all mine. I own everything as far as you can see in that direction."

Then he turned to the east, and pointed to huge herds of cattle and said again, "It's all mine, everything as far as you can see in that direction is mine." One final time he turned toward the west and pointed to a great forest and said again, "Twenty-five years ago I was penniless, but I worked hard and saved, and today I own everything as far as you can see in this direction, that direction, that direction, and this direction."

He paused for the expected praise, but to his astonishment it didn't come. Dr. Truett laid his hand lovingly on his shoulder, pointed upward and said, "My friend, how much do you own in that direction?"

Where do you turn when God says no? Do you have a relationship with him that will sustain you through the periods of life that He says no? Do you run to the arms of disillusionment or to the embrace of God? We, like David, need to look up and depend solely on our Father to give us guidance.

GRACE IN A BARREN PLACE

II Samuel 9

David asked, 'Is there still anyone left of the house of Saul to whom I may show kindness for Jonathan's sake?' Now there was a servant of the house of Saul whose name was Ziba, and he was summoned to David. The king said to him, 'Are you Ziba?' And he said, 'At your service!' The king said, 'Is there anyone remaining of the house of Saul to whom I may show the kindness of God?' Ziba said to the king, 'There remains a son of Jonathan; he is crippled in his feet.' The king said to him, 'Where is he?' Ziba said to the king, 'He is in the house of Machir son of Ammiel, at Lo-debar.' Then King David sent and brought him from the house of Machir son of Ammiel, at Lo-debar. Mephibosheth son of Jonathan son of Saul came to David, and fell on his face and did obeisance. David said, 'Mephibosheth! He answered, 'I am your servant.' David said to him, 'Do not be afraid, for I will show you kindness for the sake of your father Jonathan; I will restore to you all the land of your grandfather Saul, and you yourself shall eat at my table always.' He did obeisance and said, 'What is your servant, that you should look upon a dead dog such as I am?'

Napoleon, the great French dictator of the nineteenth century, is reported to have had a very important person on his staff who was a marginal idiot. Before every military conquest, Napoleon would write out his commands for the assault and would give this piece of paper to the idiot and ask him to read it and tell him what it said. If he could tell him what it said he would give it to his commanders and proceed with the assault. If not, he would re-write the orders.

Grace is a concept that the simplest of minds can understand. Yet, we have been guilty of making it much too complicated. Grace is the most basic element to salvation. It means gift. It is God giving us something we don't deserve. Through faith we except this gift of salvation from God.

We have expanded the basic meaning of grace. We observe a graceful pirouette by a ballerina. We admire people who gracefully carry themselves with charm and poise. We envy the ball players who gracefully make their moves when they waltz into the end zone. Music's most delicate notes are tagged with the word grace.

Listen to these words about grace by Frederick Buechner from *Wishful Thinking*:

> After centuries of handling and mishandling, most religious words have become so shopworn nobody's much interested anymore. Not so with grace, for some reason. Mysteriously, even derivatives like gracious and graceful still have some of the bloom left.
>
> Grace is something you can never get but only be given. There's no way to earn it or deserve it or bring it about any more than you can deserve the taste of raspberry and cream or earn good looks or bring about your own birth.
>
> A good sleep is grace and so are good dreams. Most tears are grace. The smell of rain is grace. Somebody loving you is grace. Loving somebody is grace.
>
> A crucial eccentricity of the Christian faith is the assertion that people are saved by grace. There's nothing you have to do. There's nothing you have to do. There's nothing you have to do.
>
> The grace of God means something like: Here is your life. You might never have been, but you are because the party wouldn't have been complete without you. Here is the world. Beautiful and terrible things will happen. Don't be afraid. I am with you. Nothing will separate us. It's for you I created the universe. I love you.
>
> There's only on catch. Like any gift, the gift of grace can be yours only if you'll reach out an take it.
>
> Maybe being able to reach out an take it is a gift too.
>
> Grace is God snatching us from a barren place, snatching us from a dry, desolate life of sin and setting us to eat from the bounty of his table. It is undeserved and unrepayable . . . it is free.

Nestled in the Old Testament in Second Samuel 9 is an example of grace. It is the story of David and Mephibosheth, Jonathan's lame son. David patterned his heart after God's by extending acceptance and mercy to a shriveled soul. It was a refreshing rain of grace to Mephibosheth.

In this story we find some characteristics of one who lives a graceful life. The grace of God so affected David's life that he lived a graceful life. He gave the gift of grace to others which he had received from God. What are the characteristics of grace that David had in his life? If you have received grace from God which characteristics do you lack? Let's take a look.

The first characteristic of grace is loyalty. Still enjoying a peaceful interlude, David begins to reflect on the promises he made to Saul and Jonathan before he was crowned king.

In eastern dynasties, when a new king took over it was common for him to kill every member of his predecessor's family. When Jonathan first heard that David would succeed his father to the throne, he asked him to spare his descendants. So David extended a hand of grace and made a covenant with Jonathan. Jonathan says:

> Thou shalt not only while I live show me the kindness of the Lord, but also thou shalt not cut off thy kindness from my house forever . . . (I Samuel 20:14-15)

David did not have to keep his promise to Jonathan. Jonathan was dead and no one would have ever known the difference. Yet, the grace of God so permeated David's life he could not be anything else but loyal.

Loyalty seems to be very rare at times. A soldier who defends his/her country in the easy times and deserts in hard times is not loyal. A husband and father who loves his wife and children when all is well and runs away for "greener grass" is bad times is not loyal. A church member who always seems to hunt something to pick at and criticize is not loyal. Loyalty means that whatever comes and whatever happens I can be depended upon.

There is one prime example of loyalty. The example of loyalty that is provided by man's best friend, the dog.

While practicing law, George G. Vest, a former United States Senator from Missouri, defended a farmer whose dog was involved in a minor damage suit. Here is part of his speech:

> The one absolutely unselfish friend that a man has in an selfish world, the one that never proves ungrateful or treacherous, is his

dog. When all other friends desert, he remains. When riches take wings and reputation falls to pieces, he is as constant in his love as the sun in its journey through the heavens.

If fortune drives the master forth and outcast in the world, friendless and homeless, the faithful dog asks no higher privilege than that of accompanying him to guard against danger, to fight against his enemies.

And, when the last scene of all comes, and death takes the master in his embrace and his body is laid away in the cold ground, no matter if all other friends pursue their way, there by the graveside will be found the noble dog, his head between his paws, his sad eyes alert and watchful, still faithful and true even in death.

With this impassioned plea, Vest won a favorable verdict from the jury.

The second characteristic of grace is it is unconditional. A person of grace does not show partiality. David called one of Saul's servants, whose name was Ziba, and asked him an intriguing question:

Is there not yet anyone of the house of Saul to whom I may show the kindness of God. (II Samuel 9:3)

Notice that David asks for anyone. Not anyone worthy or anyone qualified, but is there anyone? David's kindness was unconditional and free.

Ziba said to the king, "There is still a son of Jonathan who is crippled in both feet." Between the lines of Ziba's answer lies some cautious counsel. "You'd better think twice before you do this, David. This guy is not very kingly; he doesn't really fit the surroundings. He's a crippled, David . . . he's on crutches"

So the king said to his servant, Where is he? And Ziba said to the king, Behold, he is in the house of Machir the son of Ammiel in Lo-debar." (II Samuel 9:4)

God's grace had been extended to David unconditionally so that David wanted to give this grace to someone unconditionally.

There is a tradition that Jonathan Edwards, the third president of Princeton and one of America's greatest religious thinkers, had a daughter with an ungovernable temper. But, as is so often the case, this infirmity was not known to the outside world.

A worthy young man fell in love with this daughter and sought her had in marriage. "You can't have her," was the abrupt answer of Jonathan Edwards. "But I love her," the young man replied. "You can't have her, "said Edwards. "But she loves me!" replied the young man.

Again Edwards said, "You can't have her." "Why?" Said the young man, "Because she is not worthy of you." "But," he asked, "She is Christian is she not?" "Yes, she is a Christian, but the grace of God can live with some people with whom no one else could ever live."

The third characteristic of grace is that it is unexpected.

Let's briefly at the background of Mephibosheth. In Second Samuel 4:4 we first hear the pitiful story of Mephibosheth's injury.

> And Jonathan, Saul's son, had a son who was lame in his feet. He was five years old when the tidings came of Saul and Jonathan out of Jezreel, and his nurse took him up, and fled; and it came to pass as she made haste to flee, that he fell, and became lame. And his name was Mephibosheth.

Mephibosheth had now grown to be a man. He lived in the area call Lo-Debar which means a place without cedars or a barren place. More than likely, he was in hiding from the new king who would execute him. After all, he was a "shameful crippled". He deserved nothing more than death.

But, something unexpected happened. He received grace from the new king. As Mephibosheth approached the king he heard these words:

> Fear not; for I will surely show thee kindness for Jonathan, thy father's sake. (II Samuel 9:7)

Listen to these words by Julie Martin:

> I was that Mephibosheth
> Crippled by my twisted pride and
> hiding from You in a barren place
> where You could not find me
> where You would not give me what I deserved.
> But somehow You found me and
> I don't understand why but You

gave me what I do not deserve
You not only spared my desolate life but
You made it bountiful
And here at Your table
I will thank You my King.

The fourth characteristic of grace is that it takes a chance. Not only was Mephibosheth Jonathan's son, he was Saul's grandson. Would he be a loyal friend as was Jonathan or would he be a raging as was Saul. Nevertheless David took a chance.

God took a chance on me. He accepted me into His family not knowing if I would remain a friend or if I would become an enemy. Do you know what? He's still taking a chance on me!

Marvelous grace of our loving Lord, grace that exceeds our sin and our guilt. Yonder on Calvary's mount outpoured, there where the blood of the lamb was spilt. Grace, grace, God's grace. Grace that is greater than all our sin.

KEN STARR AND KING DAVID

II Samuel 11

In the spring of the year, the time when kings go out to battle, David sent Joab with his officers and all Israel with him; they ravaged the Ammonites, and besieged Rabbah. But David remained at Jerusalem.

It happened, late one afternoon, when David rose from his couch and was walking about on the roof of the king's house, that he saw from the roof a woman bathing; the woman was very beautiful. David sent someone to inquire about the woman. It was reported, 'This is Bathsheba daughter of Eliam, the wife of Uriah the Hittite.' So David sent messengers to fetch her, and she came to him, and he lay with her. (Now she was purifying herself after her period.) Then she returned to her house. The woman conceived; and she sent and told David, 'I am pregnant.'

When the Holy Spirit painted the portraits of Scripture's heroes, He was an artist of pure realism. He refused to brush with high-gloss colors the darker sides of their lives. The bright hues of faith and the somber shades of failure complete the picture of David.

Why doesn't the Bible gloss over the undesirable characteristics of the life of one of its greatest heroes? Wouldn't it have been easy for the writer of II Samuel to have a case of convenient amnesia with this story? The reason for the account of this story is not hard to find. The Bible is concerned to maintain the glory of God, not of any individual human being, whatever his earthly fame, his trappings, or his title.

As we look at this shameful episode of David's life, we should not shake our fingers at David's shame. We must heed the counsel of I Corinthians 10:12 which says:

Let him who thinks he stands take heed lest he should fall.

Even though this episode of David's life deals with a sexual sin, we must realize that the text gives us principles that apply to all forms of sin. It is a tendency to see sin as strictly sexual sins when sin attacks us from all areas of life. Sin also includes oppression of people, attitudes of hate and bitterness, political programs of injustice and warfare and on and on. Sin is widespread and far reaching and most of all, destructive.

The sequence of events is worthy of comment. It is human nature to shift blame for personal sin to that well worn scapegoat "combination of circumstances." In this instance it might be argued thus: Had the Ammonites not rejected David's sincere offer of a renewed treaty of peace, there would have been no war; had there been no war, Uriah would have remained at home, and David's strong initial temptation would have had no opportunity to bring forth the sinful act.

We are always paraphrasing the excuse of Adam and saying, "My life circumstances which you gave me tempted me and I did eat!" Life always offers an abundant opportunity for sin to the sinful. The opportunity to stumble is always present, but sin trips up only the sinner. We are creatures of free will. We decide upon which track our life will be placed.

The story of David and Bathsheba is a story of the most gripping kind. David was around 50 years old and had been king for about 20 years. It was spring when all the kings went forth to battle. David sent Joab and his soldiers to war against the Ammonite. David chose to stay home and let his men do all the fighting for him.

One evening, just before dark, David decided to talk a walk on the roof, much like you and I would sit on our front porch. As he looked around his great city he saw a most interesting site, Bathsheba taking her evening bath. The scripture says she was a bathing beauty.

The story continues as David inquired about this beautiful woman that he had seen. He discovers that she is married to one of Israel's chief commanders, Uriah. David sends for her to come to the palace and she and David enjoy an evening together. Soon after this evening it became apparent that nature had trapped them in sin. Bathsheba had conceived.

Instead of leaving well enough alone, the plot of the story thickens as David devises a plan to protect his kingly state as well as the reputation of Bathsheba and Uriah. David commanded Joab to bring Uriah from the battle so that he could spend some time alone with Bathsheba.

Uriah was a loyal soldier, however. Instead of going home to be with his wife he slept at the door of David's cedar house with the rest of the guard. When David found out that Uriah had slept outside of the palace he asked Uriah why he didn't go down to his own house. Uriah responded by saying:

> The ark, and Israel, and Judah abide in tents; and my lord Joab, and the servants of my lord, are encamped in the open fields. Shall, I, then, go into mine house, to eat and drink, and to lie with my wife? As thou livest, and as thy soul liveth, I will not do this thing. (II Samuel 11:11)

David's hands must have been wringing by now. He asks Uriah, why don't you stay a while in town before you go back to battle? Stay a couple of days if you want. To David's dismay Uriah still did not go to see Bathsheba. The sinful king had been rebuked by the integrity of one of his soldiers.

Then David tries to cover up one sin with another. He sends Uriah with a written message to Joab telling him to place Uriah on the front line of the hottest battle and to retreat so that Uriah would be killed. The plan, of course, worked. Uriah was now dead.

When David heard about the death of Uriah he had a-win-some-you-lose-some attitude. He says to Joab:

> Let not this thing displease thee, for the sword devoureth one as well as another. (II Samuel 11:25)

David went and fetched Bathsheba and they were married and had a son and they lived happily . . . no not quite. David had all of his tracks covered, except one. The last words in the story are haunting:

> The thing that David had done displeased the Lord. (II Samuel 11:27)

This is certainly a story of intrigue and suspense. It has the ingredients of the best of soap operas and mini—series. Yet, it has not been placed in scripture for our entertainment. It is here so that we can better prepare ourselves for sin's attack upon our life. Sin attacks us at certain times. The image of sin portrayed in Genesis is that sin couches at our doors waiting for prey. What are the windows of vulnerability in our life of which we need to be aware if we are to prevent sin's attack on us? When do we need to be most aware of sin's attack in our life, lest we, too, fall?

First—We are vulnerable to sin's attack when we have it all. When we think we are not vulnerable, we are vulnerable.

David had had a brilliant military career. He had virtually wiped out all of his serious foes. The Philistines had retreated from the Jerusalem area and David had securely established his kingdom. David had reached the pinnacle of his life. He had made it. He had reached the peak of public admiration. He enjoyed an endless supply of money, power, and fame. Never are we more vulnerable than when we have it all, and David was no exception.

Second—We are most vulnerable to sin's attack when we have time on our hands. Perhaps David placed too much stock in his track record. He began to sit back in his easy chair and let others tend to his kingly responsibilities. While David's men were in battle, he was home in bed, cushioned by royal comforts.

Our greatest battles don't come when we are out working hard, they come when we have time on our hands. It is the warm springtime when we are yawning and stretching with boredom that we make those fateful decisions that end up haunting us. Dietrich Bonhoeffer in, *Temptation*, say this about sin:

In our members there is a slumbering inclination towards desire which is both sudden and fierce. With irresistible power desire seizes mastery over the flesh. All at once a secret, smoldering fire is kindled. The flesh burns and is in flames. It makes no difference whether it is sexual desire, or ambition, or vanity, or desire for revenge, or love of fame and power, or greed for money, or, finally, that strange desire for the beauty of the world, of nature. Joy in God is . . . extinguished in us and we seek all our joy in the creature. At this moment God is quite unreal to us, he loses all reality, and only desire for the creature is real; the only reality if the devil. Satan does not fill us with hatred of God, but with forgetfulness of God . . . it is here that everything within me rises up against the Will of God.

Third—We are most vulnerable to sin's attack when we forget the consequences of sin. No doubt the stolen water of David and Bathsheba's sin was sweet, but the consequences soon turned it bitter and the taste lingered on their lips for a lifetime. Nature trapped them in their sin.

Satan never tells the heavy drinker that tomorrow there will be a hangover. He never tells the embezzler that indictment and punishment is sure. He never tells the drug addict that overdose is a likelihood. He never tells about the pain and destruction of sin. He lures you and when it is time to reap the consequences he is gone.

When you're in the heat of temptation, remember what the real consequences of sin will be—they will change, if not destroy, your life forever.

Fourth—We are vulnerable to sin's attack when we think no one will know and we can cover it up. Sin is like quicksand, the more energetic the human effort to extricate oneself the deeper the involvement.

What started out to be an innocent night of pleasure for David spread into a cover up that included murder. If he had snuffed out the spark of temptation before it began to burn out of control, his and Bathsheba's life would not have been charred and marked as it was.

Fifth, We are most vulnerable to sin's attack when we think we can hide from God. All had been covered except David's relationship with God. God was displeased.

David had managed to cover his sin up before his soldiers and before his nation, but not before God.

As we face temptation we should heed the words of Psalm 139:

> Search me, O God, and know my heart, try me and know my thoughts, and if their be any wicked way in me and lead me in the way everlasting.

SIN'S RED LIGHT

II Samuel 12

Nathan said to David, 'You are the man! Thus says the Lord, the God of Israel: I anointed you king over Israel, and I rescued you from the hand of Saul; I gave you your master's house, and your master's wives into your bosom, and gave you the house of Israel and of Judah; and if that had been too little, I would have added as much more. Why have you despised the word of the Lord, to do what is evil in his sight? You have struck down Uriah the Hittite with the sword, and have taken his wife to be your wife, and have killed him with the sword of the Ammonites. 10Now therefore the sword shall never depart from your house, for you have despised me, and have taken the wife of Uriah the Hittite to be your wife. 11Thus says the Lord: I will raise up trouble against you from within your own house; and I will take your wives before your eyes, and give them to your neighbor, and he shall lie with your wives in the sight of this very sun. For you did it secretly; but I will do this thing before all Israel, and before the sun.' David said to Nathan, 'I have sinned against the Lord.' Nathan said to David, 'Now the Lord has put away your sin; you shall not die. Nevertheless, because by this deed you have utterly scorned the Lord, the child that is born to you shall die.' Then Nathan went to his house.

The long, bony finger of Nathan the Prophet pointed to David. His sinful deed was done. Scandalous whispers buzzed throughout the palace, but no one dared say a word to the king. His pregnant bride was a mute reminder of that fateful spring night when adultery stained the king's record. Not only adultery but murder and hypocrisy and deception and a hushed cover up. The sin that had been committed was now in the open and it must be dealt with.

Nathan confronts David in an unusual way. He tells a story.

> There were two men in one city, the one rich and the other poor. The rich man had a great many flocks and herds. But the poor man had nothing except one little ewe lamb which he bought and nourished; and it grew up with him and his children. It would eat of his bread and drink of his cup and lie in his bosom, and was like a daughter to him.
>
> Now a traveler came to the rich man, and he was unwilling to take from his own flock or his own herd, to prepare for the wayfarer who had come to him; rather he took the poor man's ewe lamb and prepared it for the man who had come to him. (II Samuel 12:1-4)

Quick and powerful, David's response was like lightning tearing though a clear black night.

> As the Lord liveth, the man who hath done this thing shall surely die; and he shall restore the lamb fourfold, because he hath done this thing, and because he had no pity. (II Samuel 12:5-6)

In that vulnerable moment, David was trapped by his own reaction. Then Nathan thrusts through David's heart the sharp edged words of truth. "Thou art the Man!"

While David kept his secret, his conscience kept him bound in a straitjacket of guilt. It wasn't until Nathan confronted him that he repented, open and broken before God.

David's sin had crushing effects upon his life. The adulterous act, the murderous scheme, the hypocritical words, David committed them all behind the closed door of secrecy. Not only were they done secretly, they were done willfully. The whole tangled web of sin was woven by David's own hand. Yet, while David kept his sin hidden from the eyes of others, God saw it all.

But the thing that David had done was evil in the sight of the Lord. (II Samuel 11:27b)

Psalm 32 is a psalm of David which describes his feelings in his unrepentant state. Notice the words:

> When I kept silent about my sin, my body wasted away through my groaning all day long. For Day and night Thy hand was heavy upon me; My vitality was drained away as with the fever heat of summer. (Psalm 32:3-4)

One psychologist describes guilt as the red light on our internal dashboard. When you see the light's feverish glare, you have a choice to make. You can either pull over, get out of the car, open the hood and see what's wrong; or you can smash the light with a hammer and keep driving.

The first option leads to fixing the problem; it makes you aware of the broken water hose or the cracked radiator or the low oil level. The second only relieves the symptoms. You may be able to keep the light from glaring, but after a few more miles, serious harm could be down.

How do you treat guilt's red light? Do you take it seriously, stopping to analyze why it is flashing? Or do you smash it with the hammer you conveniently keep in the glove compartment of your conscience? Let's look at how David dealt with his guilt. How can we receive forgiveness from our sin as David did.

First—We must have an open and unguarded admission of our sin. Notice that David made such an admission without any if's, and's or but's. He said, "I have sinned against the Lord."

Do you have an unconfessed sin in your life about which you need to open and unguarded?

Second—We must desire to make a complete break from our sin. We should not only be sorry that we were caught in sin but we should be sorry and repentant of the sin itself. David had the desire to separate himself from his sin. He said:

> Purge me with hyssop, and I shall be clean; wash me, and I shall be whiter than snow. (Psalm 51:7)

Third—We must trust God for forgiveness and acceptance. God did not condemn David although he had done wrong in his sight. God saw that

David was repentant with a broken spirit and God's steadfast love reached out once again to him.

We come now to another place and time when God's steadfast love has confronted sin, our sin. On the cross Jesus took upon him the penalty of our sin. He met us so we would have the forgiveness from God. This table represents what Christ did for you and me.

As we come to the table let us openly and unguardedly say, "God, I am a sinner. Give unto me your grace which will cleanse me from my sin."

A SONG OF TRIUMPH

II Samuel 22

David spoke to the Lord the words of this song on the day when the Lord delivered him from the hand of all his enemies, and from the hand of Saul. He said:

> The Lord is my rock, my fortress, and my deliverer,
> my God, my rock, in whom I take refuge,
> my shield and the horn of my salvation,
> my stronghold and my refuge,
> my savior; you save me from violence.
> I call upon the Lord, who is worthy to be praised,
> and I am saved from my enemies.

The words of eighteenth century English dramatist William Congreve sound a truth that touches us all:

> Music has charm to soothe a savage breast, To soften rocks, or bend a knotted oak.

From an infant whose hot, tear-streaked face is cooled by a mother's tender lullaby to a corporate ladder-climbing executive whose stiff deadlines are suppled by the sweet strains of Tchaikovsky—music works its healing power in all of us.

Ira Sankey, music director for D. L. Moody, was traveling by steamboat when asked to sing "Shepherd's Song", which we know as "Savior, Like a Shepherd Lead Us." After he concluded his solo a rough looking, weather beaten man walked up and asked Sankey if he had served in the Union army. Sankey replied that he did. "Can you remember serving on picket duty on a clear spring night in 1862?" asked the man. Astonished, Sankey said, "Why, yes I did."

"So did I," continued the man, "But I was in the Confederate army. When I saw you standing at your post, I decided that you would be an easy target and that I was going to shoot you. I loaded my musket and took aim and suddenly you began to sing. Being a lover of music I decided to wait to pull the trigger. As I listened to your song, my heart began to melt. I remember the very words you sang: 'We are thine do thou befriend us, be the guardian of my way.' I became acutely aware that my relationship with God was not right.

"When you finished the song, I dropped the musket by my side and walked away."

Music's ability to soothe our terror, soften our hard spots, and bend our rigid, gnarled souls is nothing new. David, the king, besides being a warrior, shepherd, and a man of valor, was a skilled musician. He had an amazing ability to pen wonderful words to the tunes he sang.

II Samuel 22 is a beautiful example of his musicianship. Now in his twilight years, the long shadows of age and pressure stretched across his life. He had experienced several difficult events that have brought him to his knees before God: he lost his son Absalom; a severe famine struck the land; and war with Philistia was rekindled.

Weary from his struggles, David found rest in God's faithful care and he composed a triumphant song. We will find four themes from his hymn of praise to God, his deliverer.

The first theme is this—When times are tough, the Lord is our only security. To describe the difficult times which he had lived David uses words like violence, waves of death, torrents of destruction, distress, and calamity. Listen to his words:

> The Lord is my rock and my fortress and my deliverer; My God, my rock, in whom I take refuge; My shield and the horn of my salvation, my stronghold and my refuge; My savior, Thou dost save me from violence. He delivered me from my strong enemy, From those who hated me. (II Samuel 22:2-3;18-19)

David had realized that early on that God and God alone was worthy of his allegiance. God had supported David in his time of despair and he would do so in the future. Our life, too, must revolve around God if we expect this support.

"A" above middle "C" is tuned at 440 vibrations per second. Piano tuners first tune "A" before they continue with the rest of the notes. If "A" is tuned incorrectly the rest of the keyboard will be wrong.

The same is true with our relationship with God. If God is not priority one in our life all other areas will be out of line. If our heart is to pulse to the heartbeat of God then we must place God first.

Are times difficult for you? Are you running from the enemy of loneliness or pain. God will shelter you. He will take care of you. He will give you security when times are tough.

The second theme is—When days are dark, the Lord is our only light. Even in his darkest days, David found a lamp to light his way.

> For thou art my lamp, O Lord; and the Lord illumines my darkness.
> (II Samuel 22:29)

Carrying a lantern into the forest's night will not guarantee you will see all of the trees. You can be assured that you will see far enough to keep your footing sure. Likewise, as the Lord lights our path, He may not shine on all of the answers to the shadowy questions in our minds. He will give light to guide us to scale life's obstacles with confidence.

Is their fear in your life? Do you fear tomorrow? Are you afraid of failure? the unknown? Do you fear losing someone? God's light is yours. He is a shield for all who take refuge in him.

The third theme is—When our walk is weak, the Lord is our only strength. David was by no means a strong man in and of himself. In fact, when he was ruled by his own passions his character was cracked, chipped and flawed. The key to David's strength was that he acknowledged God as its source. He says:

> God is my fortress; and he sets the blameless in His way. He makes
> my feet like hinds' feet, and sets me on my high places. He trains
> my hands for battle, So that my arms can bend a bow of bronze.
> (II Samuel 22:33-35)

If you were to take a piece of hemp in your hand you would find that it is easily broken, fragile and tender. If you wrap it around other hemp it becomes a strong rope. When we twist and bend and stretch our life around God's strength we become strong.

The fourth theme is—When our future is foggy, the Lord is our only hope. As David finished his song he showed that his heart was not bitter but soft and focused upon his wonderful Lord. He was filled with the hope of God's deliverance, loving kindness and protection. He says:

> Therefore I will give thanks to Thee, O Lord, among the nations, and I will sing praise to thy name. He is a tower of deliverance to His king, and shows us loving-kindness to His anointed . . . (II Samuel 22:50-51)

The old song says it well:

> I have found a deep peace that I have never known and a joy this world cannot afford, Since I yielded control of my body and soul to my wonderful, wonderful Lord.

The future is intended to be the brightest portion of our life. Sometimes it's foggy. Behind the clouds of darkness, we can depend upon God being there. We may be unsure about the future but we can be sure about who holds it.

We don't have to wait to the end of our life to discover God's care for us. We don't have to wait until pressure and stress overtake us. We can discover these themes now!

Are there tough times in your life? Have you been through some dark days? Are you about to crumble? Is your future foggy and frightening? Only the Lord of security . . . light . . . strength . . . and hope can see you through. Won't you cling closely to this wonderful Lord and make David's song of triumph your own?

WHEN DAVID GOOFED

II Samuel 24

Again the anger of the Lord was kindled against Israel, and he incited David against them, saying, 'Go, count the people of Israel and Judah.' So the king said to Joab and the commanders of the army, who were with him, 'Go through all the tribes of Israel, from Dan to Beer-sheba, and take a census of the people, so that I may know how many there are.' But Joab said to the king, 'May the Lord your God increase the number of the people a hundredfold, while the eyes of my lord the king can still see it! But why does my lord the king want to do this?' But the king's word prevailed against Joab and the commanders of the army. So Joab and the commanders of the army went out from the presence of the king to take a census of the people of Israel. They crossed the Jordan, and began from Aroer and from the city that is in the middle of the valley, towards Gad and on to Jazer. Then they came to Gilead, and to Kadesh in the land of the Hittites; and they came to Dan, and from Dan they went round to Sidon, and came to the fortress of Tyre and to all the cities of the Hivites and Canaanites; and they went out to the Negeb of Judah at Beer-sheba. So when they had gone through all the land, they came back to Jerusalem at the end of nine months and twenty days. Joab reported to the king the number of those who had been recorded: in Israel there were eight hundred thousand soldiers able to draw the sword, and those of Judah were five hundred thousand.

The newspaper headlines of the last week or so have provided us with some interesting topics for discussion:

MINISTER INDICTED ON CHILD SEX CHARGE
WILT'S ACTIONS DEADLY
MAGIC JOHNSON TESTS POSITIVE TO HIV TEST
PARENTS ON TRIAL FOR ABUSE BECAUSE OF RELIGION
ORAL ROBERTS URGES DONATION FOR SATANIC
    CONSPIRACY
RELIGION ISSUE ADDING FIRE TO GOVERNOR'S RACE
BAPTISTS WAGE POLITICAL WARS

We all agree that these headlines represent the bad that is done around us. The interesting thing is that the headlines represent our society's "cream of the crop" people. To many people these "good" people are heroes. Heroes who have fallen. Good people who have done bad things.

These events remind me of Chaucer's statement: If the gold rusts, what will the iron do?

The Bible is full of headlines like these. King David had a few of his own.

David was paradox personified. He Slew Goliath with a fling of a stone yet he was wounded by his wandering eyes. He soothed Saul's spirit with smooth soft strains on his harp yet he exploded with anger at Nabal. He gave Jonathan's crippled son grace, a place a the royal table yet he ignored the needs of his own children. He hid from God yet he knew how to draw near to him.

II Samuel 24 is an occasion where David Goofed. He messed up . . . again. What he did was not wrong in and of itself but it sounded some chords that did not sound as if they came from one whose life pulsed to the heartbeat of God.

One reason I know the Bible is true it does not cover the blemishes of its heroes. God does not hire a Public Relations firm to put a good spin on their lives. The Bible describes them warts and all. David not any other person, idea or movement was to be placed upon a pedestal. He was human. He was sinful. He was like you and me—God loved him and he loved God.

Most children outgrow their foolish ways. They mature and shed the name calling and the my-dad-is-bigger-than-your-dad mentality. Sadly, as God's children we never outgrow our capability to mess things up. We think we are big enough to take the training wheels off and we fall. We try to have it our way and we goof up.

Today we see David, gray at his ruddy temples, make a foolish decision based on pride, the consequences of which were staggering. It reminds us of the seriousness of taking things into our own hands. We find David in the latter years of his reign. He was on the heals of a Philistine—Israeli war. A series of skirmishes had taken place where David and soldiers had killed more giants from Gath. Fresh from victory, David was vulnerable. Wanting to reinforce his sense of military security and pride, David commanded Joab to make a census. Joab knew something was awry and questioned David. David arrogantly ignored inquiry and went full steam ahead. Sin found an opening in David's mind. It found a crack in his character that pride had created and it moved him to commit another tragic act. Joab finished the census and found that there were 1.3 million men in Israel and Judah.

What was so wrong with what David did? What harm would it be to count the men of Israel and Judah? Nothing except it was not what God wanted of him. David again went rough shod ahead, leaving God out of his life, headed straight for trouble. David knew what would happen.

King David was old enough to know better. God dealt with him more harshly because his experience had proven that doing things out of God's will would lead to disaster. Let's let at what the story teaches us today.

First—It teaches us that we must trust in God and not man. David wanted to see how much military power he had. He knew that it didn't matter about Man's power. It mattered about God's power. Nevertheless, he counted.

Napoleon once said, "God is on the side of the heaviest artillery. However this proved to be wrong at Waterloo where Napoleon had 250 guns whereas the English had 150. Reverend Parkhurst said at the beginning of a fierce battle, "Gentlemen, it looks dark, but God is on our side, and how much do you count him for?"

Are you facing difficulty? Are their storms in your life? Are temptations assaulting you? You can depend on the power of the presence of God!

Second—It teaches us that we must stay in touch with the Lord. In this story we do not see where David prayed or sought God. He simply did it.

How many times have you bought something and dived head first into assembling it without reading the instructions? Finally, at wits end you look at the directions.

Leslie Stokes, an English Baptist Minister tells this parable:

Once Upon a Time there was a tree, a very lovely tree. It was strong, shapely and stately. The tree knew inwardly that its massive strength was beginning to wane. When the wind blew it could feel the sway more and more. It would hear suspicious creaks, So, wisely, it took itself in hand and with much effort began to grow new branches. It looked stronger and safer than ever. The next gale blew and the was a terrific snapping in the roots of the tree. But for the support of a friendly neighbor, it would have fallen.

When the tree recovered from the shock, it asked the neighbor how it was able to stand its ground and was able to help it stand, too. The neighbor responded by saying, "When you were busy growing branches, I was strengthening my roots!"

Are you more concerned with your outward strength than you inward strength? Do you concentrate on what people think of you rather than on what God's thinks? We must stay in touch with God so deep roots of faith will grow to support us in difficult times.

Third—It teaches us that we must be accountable to others. David was nestled in his ivory tower. Having reached a peerless position, David answered to no one. He was king! When he rested in the security of his position he found himself in trouble.

Jimmy Swaggart this fallacy so eloquently a week or so ago when he said: "The Holy Spirit rolled me over and told me that it was none of the church's business what he did." We are accountable to each other.

If you find yourself in the trusted position of unquestioned authority, watch out. Life on the pedestal is precarious. When you fall from the heights, you not only fall hard, you shatter those beneath you. Don't live life unchecked. Surround yourself with people who will put integrity on the pedestal—not you.

Fourth—It teaches us that we should not forget sin's consequences. The consequence of this goof was tremendous. It cost 70,000 their lives.

We should never forget the serious of sin. Billy Sunday said, "I'm against sin. I'll kick it as long as I've got a foot. I'll fight it as long as I've got a fist. I'll butt it as long as I've got a head. I'll bite it as long as I got a tooth. When

I'm old and fistless and footless and toothless, I'll Gum it until I go home to glory and it goes home to perdition."

Fifth—It teaches us that we are all capable of gross misconduct. If a man as faithful as King David fell into sins grasp, we can too. There is probably a thought, idea or concept that has the capability of destroying us.

Are you heading toward a mistake? Are you about to goof? Have you consulted with God and asked for his guidance? God wants to lead and to guide. Won't you let him have his way with you?

THE END OF AN ERA

I Chronicles 28-29

Thus David son of Jesse reigned over all Israel. The period that he reigned over Israel was forty years; he reigned for seven years in Hebron and thirty-three years in Jerusalem. He died at a good old age, full of days, riches, and honor; and his son Solomon succeeded him. Now the acts of King David, from first to last, are written in the records of the seer Samuel, and in the records of the prophet Nathan, and in the records of the seer Gad, with accounts of all his rule and his might and of the events that befell him and Israel and all the kingdoms of the earth.

Pete Rose stepped to the plate on April 13, 1963, and made the first hit which would chart his career as one of baseball's best players. Through his career he would break 19 major league records including Ty Cobb's batting record of 4,000 hits. At the end of his playing career he amassed 4,264 hits. Sportswriters would agree that he is one of the greatest baseball players that ever played the game.

Baseball Commissioner A. Bartlett Giamoti, banned him from the game for life because of illegal activity centering around baseball. He stated, "No one will be bigger than the game."

In a press conference, Pete Rose said, "Baseball is my life." For thirty years he had centered his life around baseball. Now he was banished from the game. What did he have left? He was a pitiful sight of a person who had lived over half of his life centered around something temporal. Whether friend or foe, one would have to agree that baseball had come to an end of an era, albeit a disastrous one.

Some people mark the beginning of an era by forging new and uncharted courses, standing alone against the inevitable critics and enemies of change. Others mark the end of an era with their death. As they pass on, they leave a chasm that no one seems to be able to fill.

David, the man after God's own heart, was like that. Although his son Solomon was destined to become great, he was never really the man his father had been. In Acts we find a profound statement that underscores the significance of David's life.

> For David, after he had served the purpose of God in his own
> generation, fell asleep, and was laid among his fathers. (Acts 13:36)

David had faithfully led Israel for forty years. He fathered Solomon, God's chosen successor to the throne. In I Chronicles 28-29 we see him in the final chapter of his life. Realizing he was near death, swelling with emotion and memories, David reflected on his years as king. His death ended an era that would never be duplicated in the annals of history.

As his life draws to a close, he calls together an assembly of all his national leaders, including his son Solomon, the king—elect. In these closing pages of David life we find some valuable gems of truth. Let's take a look.

First—David addresses the national leaders. He stresses that life must be centered around God's desire rather than around our dreams. David reflects upon his unfulfilled dream. His desire was simple and pure. He had wanted to build a home for the sacred ark of the covenant.

> Then David rose to his feet and said, Listen to me, my brethren
> and my people; I had intended to build a permanent home for the
> ark of the covenant of the Lord and for the footstool of our God.
> So I had made preparations to build it. But God said to me, You
> shall not build a house for My name because you are a man of war
> and have shed blood. (I Chronicles 28:2-3)

Although the cherished ambition to build the temple was born in David, it was carried out by Solomon. David accepted God's no without a trace of bitterness and resentment. He said:

> Yet, the Lord, the God of Israel, chose me from all the house of
> my father to be king over Israel forever. For He has chosen Judah

to be leader; and in the house of Judah, my father's house, and among the sons of my father He took pleasure in me to make me king over all Israel. (I Chronicles 28:4)

Rather than pining the last few years of his life away with an ache for that unfulfilled desire, David focuses on what the Lord will allow him to do.

Has God said no to one of your dreams? Maybe a great accomplishment . . . a certain career . . . a ministry . . . a relationship? If so, relinquish it. Let it go. Focus upon what the Lord *will* do in your life instead of what he hasn't done. We must focus upon what we *can* do rather than upon what we cannot do.

Second—David addresses his son. He stresses that life must be centered around the unfailing quality of godliness. David turns his attention to his son. Solomon, inexperienced, untried, unscarred, would be the fulfillment of David's dream to build a temple.

An interesting side road is that prior to this, Absalom, his best beloved son, was the son in whom David had placed his dream. What a loving expectation he had that Absalom would be his successor. But Absalom was dead, leaving behind him a name for reckless courage and ruthless plotting to overthrow his father. David had to transfer his hopes.

I suppose one of the most difficult things in life is to transfer one's hope. Many parents know what it feels like to have great hopes for a child to do well as an adult and have the child disappoint their expectations. Many children know what it means to be disappointed by parents behavior. Friends, family, jobs all disappoint and require us to transfer our hope.

David gives Solomon some invaluable advice and he expresses this advice with three words: Know . . . Serve . . . and Seek. Know the Lord, Serve the Lord, and Seek the Lord. David instructed his son on the fine points of godliness.

Understanding the difficulties of ruling a nation, David counsels Solomon to know the Lord, to progressively become more deeply and intimately acquainted with Him, perceiving and recognizing and understanding Him more strongly and more clearly.

David tells Solomon to serve God in two ways:

And serve Him with a whole heart and a willing mind; for the Lord searches all hearts, and understands every intent of the thoughts. (I Chronicles 28:9)

David, the sweet singer of Israel, knows that God examines His children's heart and sees their every motive. When others cannot see past our self-made venire. God's sees.

David also urges his son to seek God, be sensitive to Him, listen to the nudgings of His voice. What great advice! Know . . . Serve . . . and Seek.

Finally—David addresses the people of Israel. He stresses that life must be centered around the unfailing majesty of God. Together they bless the Lord. Together they pay homage to the Lord and to the king. Then, quietly, the Scripture shines the light back on David; except now David's lamp is dim, the candle of his life is about to go out.

> Then he died in a ripe old age, full of days, riches and honor. (I Chronicles 29:28)

Like David, we all have a purpose for our lives. What has God given you as your purpose? God gifted David with political wisdom, strength, and, most importantly, a soft heart. Are you fulfilling God's purpose in your life?

> All I could never be,
> All men ignored in me,
> This, I was worth to God, whose wheel the pitcher shaped.

ABOUT THE AUTHOR

David R. Tullock is a pastor who has developed a unique approach to ministry he calls an "integrated ministry." Having many interests, his ministry expresses how he understands God has called him to serve. His partner in ministry is the congregation of Northside Presbyterian Church, Cleveland, Tennessee.

Dr. Tullock is a graduate of Carson Newman College, in Jefferson City, Tennessee and holds two graduate degrees from Southern Seminary in Louisville, Kentucky, including a Doctor of Ministry. He has had extensive training in Family Systems Theory and Death and Grief Education. He has been a popular teacher of English and Religion at Chattanooga State Technical Community College, Cleveland State Community College, Pastoral Care in the Program of Alternative Studies at Memphis Theological Seminary and Lee University. He is a gifted preacher and an engaging pastor.

Believing in social justice, Dr. Tullock has led congregations in developing and participating in various ministries which help the, those living outside the bounds of society because of sickness, grief, poverty or life-circumstances. He was founder of Rossville Community Ministry in Rossville, Georgia, which serves as a social ministry to the poor and involves over 25 churches and organizations. He is actively involved in Parson's Porch, a bereavement ministry, Habitat for Humanity and Heifer Project International.

Dr. Tullock's greatest delights in life are his wife, Cristy, and their three children, David Isaac, Sadie Grace and Lily Anne. Of all the titles he has, his favorite is Daddy.

More information about Dr. Tullock can be found at www.davidtullock.com.

Printed in Great Britain
by Amazon